THE HORROR ANTHOLOGY HANDBOOK

A FILMMAKER'S REFERENCE FOR MAKING FEATURES OUT OF SHORTS

BY KEITH TYLER HOPKINS

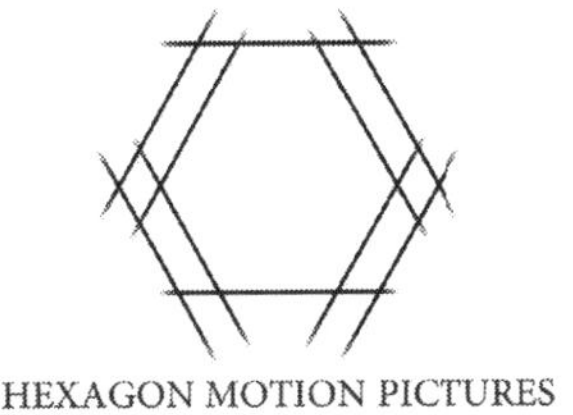

HEXAGON MOTION PICTURES

The Horror Anthology Handbook

Editing by Matthew Dressel
Cover design by Nesihan Yardimli, BookCoverZone.com

ISBN 9798686234482
First Edition: October, 2020
Published by Hexagon Motion Pictures
HexagonMotionPictures.com

This activity is made possible in part by the voters of Minnesota through a grant from the Arrowhead Regional Arts Council, thanks to appropriations from The McKnight Foundation and the Minnesota State Legislature's general and arts and cultural heritage funds.

-Sophie Gelson: What Rod Serling did was he took this silly genre kid stuff and he elevated it. He made art with it, for grown-ups…

-Jordan Peele: You don't like campfire stories?

-THE TWILIGHT ZONE, 2019

TABLE OF CONTENTS

INTRODUCTION

[HOW TO USE THIS BOOK & HORROR ANTHOLOGY 101]

It's the mid-nineties and I'm on a Boy Scout camping trip with my dad, my best friends, and their dads. The air is crisp, the fire is crackling, and we're telling ghost stories. My father had an instinct for the things many people don't consider when telling a story, like when to insert a pause and let the fire do the talking. Suddenly, the usually quiet Mr. Abrignani tells us that something's recently happened to him that he'd like to talk about. It's an absolutely true ghost story he has experienced in a house he's recently bought. It's hard to say why I became so captivated by his story, because other people had told true ghost stories at such gatherings before. Part of it must've been that, through the act of telling it to us, he seemed to be coming to a better understanding of the events himself. His story stuck with me, affected me deeply, and though I'd seldom speak of it, I'd run through it in my mind often. *That'd make a great movie*, I would think to myself.

Some fifteen years later, I reached out to Gary (I didn't have to call him Mr. Abrignani in adulthood fortunately) and asked if I could base a narrative short film around his experience. He seemed floored, not only that I'd remembered his story in the first place, but also that I was able to recite its particulars so accurately. With his blessing, and my now deceased father's knack for tone and pacing at top-of-mind, I set off on a journey that would ultimately lead me to directing my own horror anthology film, as well as authoring this book. And the significance of it all stemming from a campfire isn't lost on me.

I'm far from the first to point out that storytelling around a fire was likely the first form of communal entertainment amongst early humans. Just look to Steven Spielberg. The opening to his 80s anthology series, ***Amazing Stories***, begins with cavemen sitting around a fire swapping stories before racing through time to the modern era where a family gathers in the living room to watch those same cavemen on TV. As ***Amazing Stories*** asserts, it's from the mode of storytelling that naturally occurs at a campfire that the horror anthology gets its basic structure.

Anthologies are best defined as long-form productions, whether films or TV shows, that are compiled from short-form content. This includes feature films that are an assembly of short films, or TV shows in which each episode features a new set of characters and locations. These seemingly disparate segments are most often tied together by a framing device of some sort, whether it be Rod Serling introducing episodes of ***The Twilight Zone***, or characters telling each other stories around a fire, as in 1997's ***Campfire Tales***.

These films and TV shows basically function as such: an introductory narrative is established that is used to flow into the shorter stories. I'll refer to such segments as either "wraparounds" or "frame stories." Next in the typical anthology comes the first short film, and I'll address how various anthologies handle this transition in Section II. Here, you'll see me use the terms "segue" or "segue device," which simply refers to the methods the filmmakers are using to get from the frame story, to a short film, and back to the frame story. I'll also often write, "framing device," which refers to the tropes and methodologies being used within the frame story.

I didn't know any of this when I started making horror shorts. Inspired by the story I'd heard at the fire that night, I made my first short film based on Gary Abrignani's experience, and followed that up with three more paranormal horror shorts over the course of several years. While I knew these shorts had the potential to be career-building assets, I was unsure of what to do with them. Festivals? TV? YouTube? Vimeo? Social media? I ended up trying various release strategies to create buzz around my films, with little effect. At the time, I was fortunate enough to be working at a broadcast affiliate, which got me a connection to the local Duluth Superior Film Festival, as well as the opportunity to direct a whole lot of episodes of a show called ***Night at the Movies*** for our local CBS and CW channels. This show featured independent short films of all genres, and, needless to say, I included my own shorts. In the end though, I'd gained a lot of skills, a little bit of exposure, but little towards paying the bills with my independent filmmaking. From listening to podcasts like ***Indie Film Hustle***, I'd learned that if I want to make feature films for a living, I'd have to start by making a feature film for next to nothing. But how to go about it? Early on in the production of my shorts I decided that, with one exception, I wouldn't post them permanently online. If I held onto them, I reasoned, perhaps I could tie them all together into a feature. Though I didn't know it at the time, what I was cooking up in the back of my mind was a horror anthology film.

After seeing my shorts, several friends recommended I watch films like ***V/H/S*** and ***The ABCs of Death***. This is where the floodgates opened. I dreamt up possible concepts for an anthology film that could combine my shorts into a cohesive narrative, several of which were no good at all. It actually wasn't until I began searching for funding that a good idea for the framing device came into focus.

In 2018, I wrote a grant proposal to the Minnesota State Arts Board for $10,000 to finish my paranormal anthology, ***Gravedigger Dave's Halfway House***. What I found was that the process of writing a grant forces the applicant to narrow their artistic vision down to its most interesting concepts, and articulate the project's objectives in as succinct a way as possible. I proposed to the Arts Board that I'd make a film chronicling the area's ghost stories in a stylistic hybrid between narrative and documentary. I'll share more details on my proposal and how I got the grant in Section III, but for now all you need to know is that I had about 6 months to kill while I waited to find out if the project would be funded.

A few weeks after submitting the proposal, I was listening to ***The Indie Film Hustle Podcast*** episode 201, during which ***Story Maps*** author Daniel Calvisi encouraged filmmakers to map out the structures of films similar to the one they'd like to make. He said, "Don't just watch movies and think about them. Do written analysis…because it forces you to really take it apart." It was then that I realized I hadn't been doing my research. I'd watched some anthologies, but hadn't attempted to analyze what worked and what didn't, or the ways in which anthology filmmakers connected their short films. I began my research with the 1963 classic, ***Black Sabbath***. After realizing how much work it'd be to deconstruct an entire horror subgenre in this manner, I took to the internet looking for a book, thinking there must be an author out there that'd done the work for me. I searched high and low. Nothing.

So without a second thought, I started writing the book I wish I had read when I set out to make a horror anthology, and it's been made specifically for independent horror filmmakers. In reading this book, you'll be able to understand the approaches other anthology filmmakers have taken in order to better approach your own film. You'll hear from the editor of ***Trick 'r Treat***, an editor from ***Black Mirror***, the producer of ***V/H/S*** and ***Southbound***, a director who helmed 17 episodes of ***Are You Afraid of the Dark?*** and 16 episodes of ***Goosebumps***, the creator of ***The ABCs of Death***, and tons more. These wonderful folks all approach anthologies from a different angle, yet you'll notice common threads throughout each interview in Section I. Most importantly, they were all happy to share information you'll surely use as you make your own anthology film. I certainly did.

As connecting short films is the primary concern of this book, Section II analyzes nearly 75 films and series, ordered chronologically. Particular attention is paid to the way in which their wraparounds, pacing, and story structure are approached. The wraparounds of each are broken into a few categories:

- **Storytelling:** Characters in the frame story tell each other stories, thus leading to the short films. Used in *Tales From the Hood, Gravedigger Dave's Halfway House, Are You Afraid of the Dark?*
- **Mind's Eye:** Wraparounds in which we see a character's thoughts or dreams. Used in

Dr. Terror's House of Horrors, and *Torture Garden*.

- **Horror Host:** A character breaks the fourth wall, speaking directly to the audience, to navigate to the short films. Used in *The Twilight Zone*, *Tales From the Crypt*, and *Body Bags*.
- **Film Within a film:** Wraparounds in which polished short films are shown to an audience in the anthology. Used in *Night Train to Terror*, *Chillerama,* and *Nightmare Cinema*.
- **Found Footage:** Wraparounds that involve the discovery of short films that have a raw, unedited feel. Used in *V/H/S* and *The Dark Tapes*.
- **Package Film:** An anthology that plays out like a short film program at a festival. Used in *Twice Told Tales* and *Kwaidan*.
- **Thematic Throughline:** Shorts that are linked by tone, topic, genre, setting, or style. Used in *The ABCs of Death*, *Holidays*, and *Black Mirror*.
- **Tangential Throughline:** Anthologies in which short segments flow into and out of each other without the aid of a consistent wraparound, or with a variety of wraparound-types simultaneously. Used in

Trick 'r Treat, *Southbound*, and *Volumes of Blood.*

The above categories are geared towards helping you understand the rules so that you can break them. As ***Volumes of Blood*** creator, P.J. Starks, challenged himself, "When it comes to creating the framework for what is an anthology, how can you take something that's been done a gazillion times already and put your own spin on it to where you're not just redoing ***Tales from the Darkside*** or ***After Midnight***?" Put another way, deconstructing the horror anthology genre will help you create a structure for your film that feels fresh. That may require abandoning the traditional three-act structure that's been mapped out in many screenwriting books, like the seminal ***Save the Cat***.

What I've found in my research of anthologies is that the traditional rules of structure and character often don't apply to the subgenre. Just watch the very unconventional, yet very successful, ***ABCs of Death*** series. In movies like this, you won't find characters that have fully formed arcs, and that's just fine. Likewise, quality shorts and quality anthologies often do not have the "hero's journey" that Joseph Campbell mapped out in his ***The Hero with a Thousand Faces***. Horror anthology filmmaking frees you from such structural framework.

For further reassurance on this matter, refer to ***The Simpsons*** **"Treehouse of Horror"** Halloween specials. At the time of the writing of this book, Al Jean is the showrunner for ***The Simpsons***, and has been for more years than any other showrunner. Reaching out to someone of his stature was a real shot in the dark, and I was kind of starstruck when he told my editor he'd answer some questions over Twitter. When I asked if the vibe of the writers' room changed when crafting these annual horror-themed episodes, Jean wrote, "There's a lot of excitement among the writers and directors for the "Treehouse" episodes; some because of the horror genre but more because of the freedom of three unrelated acts which obey fewer rules and in many cases are based on a classic story." The part that really struck me from his statement was, "the freedom of three unrelated acts." I underline "unrelated" because it's indicative of a structural approach you're going to find in most, if not all, of the anthologies I write about. An anthology film only has to work on a scene by scene basis. It can lack cohesiveness as a whole, but still be a rewarding viewing experience if it functions as an ongoing series of engaging shorts.

Such shorts often fall into a variety of categories, the tropes of which I'll briefly describe here. These are generalizations meant to show patterns in anthology filmmaking throughout the years. Of course, not everything fits into a box. Nevertheless, here are a few boxes:

- **The cycle will continue:** The end of the short, in one way or another, restarts the events that began the short. This approach was popularized by *The Twilight Zone*.

- **The Twist:** We learn at the end that nothing is what we thought. Also popularized by *The Twilight Zone.*
- **This is just the beginning:** The shorts function as a setup, or world-build, for what would hypothetically be a larger story, as seen with the *Machete* trailer in *Grindhouse*.
- **The second act cutoff**: The short ends just before what could be the third act of a feature film, leaving the audience hanging.
- **Walk around slowly and die:** A protagonist who we all know is going to die walks around an empty house until something slaughters them.
- **Punchline:** The entire short builds towards a joke.
- **There was nothing to be afraid of after all:** Common in anthologies for kids, like *Goosebumps* or *Are Your Afraid of the Dark?*
- **Femme fatale:** A popular Film noir trope in which a woman who appears to be a victim winds up being a predator, as seen in *Trick 'r Treat*, *V/H/S*, *Holidays*, and more.
- **Surprise... we're on a movie set:** Oftentimes, when a short begins at what seems like the height of the tension, you can be sure that an off-camera voice is about to

yell, "cut," so that the short's real story can begin. This can be seen in *The Uncanny*, *Three... Extremes*, and more.

- **Possessed dolls:** As seen in *Trilogy of Terror*, *Tales From the Hood 2*, and many more.
- **Wishes and fortunes gone wrong:** Such shorts usually involve gypsies, visions of the future, or cursed objects, as seen in *Gravedigger Dave's Halfway House.*
- **Body horror:** A character is subjected to a sickening transformation or disfigurement. This also includes experimental medical procedures gone wrong, as well as supernatural pregnancies, as seen in *Holidays*.
- **Murder plot:** Usually for money or love, as seen in *Asylum*.
- **Cautionary tales:** Shorts where characters learn a lesson the hard way, as seen in *Creeped Out*.

These are, of course, generalizations and simplifications. There are many more types of short films in the world than what is described above. But as you keep the types of shorts most common to the form in the back of your mind, know that one of the most difficult challenges you'll face will be the ordering of shorts within your anthology. In some films, like ***The ABCs of Death*** and

Holidays, the ordering of shorts is inherent to the way in which the movie was produced, and cannot be changed in the editing room. But things are not always this set in stone. In a film series like ***V/H/S***, for instance, the short films could conceivably be edited in any order. And most filmmakers will spend a fair amount of time toiling over the order in which the shorts will appear.

If you don't believe me, consider this approach to the 2019 Netflix anthology series, ***Love Death + Robots***, as described on Twitter.

> We've never had a show like Love, Death & Robots before so we're trying something completely new: presenting four different episode orders. The version you're shown has nothing to do with gender, ethnicity, or sexual identity — info we don't even have in the first place.
>
> - Netflix US (@netflix)
> March 19, 2019

One could easily take this to mean that the ordering of shorts, in fact, does not matter, and can even be randomized. But I believe that Netflix's approach to ***Love Death + Robots*** actually proves the opposite. Undoubtedly, the streaming service will collate the analytics from the four episode orders to see which is the most successful (and by "successful" I mean which leads to the greatest amount of user-engagement.) If one performs markedly better than the others, it's reasonable to assume they'd switch to that order permanently. Would Netflix have conducted this unprecedented experiment if the ordering of stories in an anthology was not important? Of course not, and their approach is of supreme significance. Up to this point, the ordering of the shorts in an anthology was largely based on the intuition of the filmmakers, or in some cases, results from test screenings.

Robert Ivison, the editor of ***Trick 'r Treat***, told me about test screenings they conducted which led to a restructuring of their film. He said, "I think that once we put it together the way it was written and we screened it, Mike Dougherty [director], Bryan Singer [producer], and the studio said, okay we really like the crossovers. We like the way that we go back and forth between tales. Is there any way to engage the audience more by going back and forth more frequently, or maybe changing the order of the stories?"

If filmmakers at this level are toiling about the ordering of the shorts in their film, you can expect to as well. So, take a step back from the shorts you've made, or plan to make. Perhaps you have some funny ones, some bloody ones, and some slow-burning creepy ones. I'm sure you're wondering which order will make your anthology most effective. In the forthcoming interviews and film analysis, you'll learn what other filmmakers have done, and thus come to an informed conclusion about what you should do.

So why should you make a horror anthology film? For me, it meant I could make my first feature over time, short film by short film, all the while honing my craft. I took comfort in the fact that all of the work I put into each short was going towards a bigger project, and that the success (or failure) of any one of them wouldn't stop me from moving towards the ultimate goal of finishing a feature film. Doing it in this fashion meant there was no need to perfect a 90 page narrative before shooting. I was able to tackle the story in small pieces, confident that I could connect the dots later.

In that spirit, this is kind of a *Choose Your Own Adventure* book. It's meant to be browsed and skipped around. As you browse Sections I and II, I'm sure your eyes will pass over a film or two that you don't like. I'd be lying if I said I'm a fan of every film in this book, but your objective here shouldn't be to say whether a film is good or bad. There are plenty of critics in the world doing a fine job at that. Your purpose here is to learn from what other filmmakers have done, discover how and why they made their film the way they did, and use that analysis to inform your own approach.

For instance, perhaps you've been wondering whether you should direct each segment of your anthology yourself, or collaborate with other directors. That's a tough one, and your answer will depend on a lot of things. Do you want your anthology to be a showcase of your stylistic capabilities or would you rather pool your creativity with other talented folks? You'll find a plethora of examples from each side of that coin, and great insight from filmmakers on why they chose to go one way or the other. It's likely you'll find that the films you don't like will be the ones informing your decisions the most.

So what has not been included in this book? While fantastic in their storytelling, anthology series that tell their stories over several long installments, like ***True Detective***, ***American Horror Story***, or ***Welcome to the Blumhouse*** are not the concern of this book. These anthologies are more like mega-narratives than the productions I wish to deconstruct. It is the peculiarities of short-form storytelling, and the combining of those short works into a longer work that will be my focus.

A quick note on spoilers; to a certain degree, the process of analysis necessitates spoilers. I'll do my best to tease the plots of these films without giving *everything* away, but the nature of this book makes spoilers inevitable. You've been warned, but hopefully not deterred. Read about the films you have not seen and let my analysis inform your thinking when you do get around to watching them.

To bring my campfire analogy back for a moment, anthology films, in their most basic forms, are analogous to a night around the fire. During your average camping trip, someone builds a fire and folks gather around it. This is the setup of the wraparound. When a person tells a story, this is analogous to the first short films in the anthology. When a storyteller finishes, people around the fire will reflect on what's been said, until another person has a story to tell, and so the evening will go.

If this reminds you of a certain Nickelodeon TV series from the 90s, you're definitely reading the right book. The stories in ***Are You Afraid of the Dark?*** were favorites of mine growing up. But sitting in the dark woods around those fires as a kid, I listened to the scariest stories I have ever heard. As is the natural progression of things, when the nights' storytellers had run out of stories to tell, water would be used to douse the fire, sending smoke into the dark woods as the cold closed in on us. Few things have scared and fascinated me as deeply as looking out into the lonely forests of upstate New York as the last embers died, wondering what existed beyond my comprehension. Every time I turn on a movie, I'm wanting it to be the best movie I've ever watched. It's always my hope that when the credits rise like a plume of smoke, they'll leave me with the same simultaneous sense of wonder and dread. On occasion, they do. And in this book, their creators speak.

SECTION I: THE INTERVIEWS

[INSIGHTS ON TURNING SHORT FILMS INTO FEATURE FILMS]

Early into my research of horror anthology films it became clear that the *The Horror Anthology Handbook* would benefit from the insights of the folks who worked on the films and series I'd be analyzing. I reached out to a lot of people. Some never got back. Others did get back, but we were never able to lock down an interview. I was shocked, though, at the caliber of the film professionals who I did end up speaking with. Surprisingly, it seemed the folks of higher stature were more willing to do an interview than folks at the opposite end of the filmmaking food chain. Some agreed to have lengthy phone conversations with me, while others answered a few questions over email. In both cases, there's a wealth of filmmaking knowledge in the stories they share. The process of reaching out to them also taught me a valuable lesson about who might be willing to lend their time if you only ask. In general, I think people are eager to share what they have learned, and I feel privileged to share their words with you.

INTERVIEW WITH ROBERT IVISON

(TRICK 'R TREAT EDITOR)

-Background: ***Trick 'r Treat*** is, to say the least, a seminal film in the horror anthology subgenre. It is revered by fans who boast tattoos of the iconic Sam, and flock to annual screenings leading up to Halloween. I knew I had to talk to someone behind ***Trick 'r Treat***. Writer/director Michael Dougherty would be too busy for me, as he was working on the massive tentpole picture ***Godzilla: King of the Monsters*** at the time. With ***Trick 'r Treat***'s supremely unique structure, though, I thought it might be more interesting to speak with the editor anyway. Fans of Dougherty's know the film was a labor of love for him, but I hoped that speaking with Robert Ivison might offer a more objective look at the film's construction. I was not disappointed.

-Keith Tyler Hopkins: How did you get involved in editing ***Trick 'r Treat***?

-Robert Ivison: The film was already underway with another editor and I was asked to come in and help smooth some scenes out and take things over. So I came on. They were still shooting. They probably had three weeks to shoot still. It was shot in Vancouver. So I was in Vancouver for January through April of that year and then we tested it in

Los Angeles two times. So it was finished by June I think of that year, so six months.

-KTH: It seems like it was a really complex film to assemble.

-RI: It was. It was written as an anthology of stories that overlapped at particular places and times. I think that once we put it together the way it was written and we screened it, Mike Dougherty [director], and Brian Singer [producer], and the studio said, okay we really like the crossovers, we like the way that we go back and forth between tales. Is there any way to engage the audience more by going back and forth more frequently or maybe changing the order of the stories? Originally it was four distinct stories that played out in progression and overlapped at certain points. And you would realize, okay now we're on the other side of the door of the trick or treaters with the principal or now we're on the outside. Now we're seeing that scene from a different perspective. And I think they really liked that feature of it, but they wanted to enhance that. They wanted it to play in a different order. So there was some structural work that had to be done after the first preview.

Like any film you want to make it as tight as you can and take time out of it if the audience is moving around in their seats or you're feeling like, okay their minds are wandering. You need to keep them in the palm of your hand for the whole duration. And I think we succeeded in that. I know that the end product was very different structurally from how Mike had written it, but I think ultimately he was very happy with the way that audiences received it. I've been in screenings with him... and the crowd goes crazy for it.

-KTH: So in the original script did each short play out in full as its own isolated story?

-**RI:** Yes. Each chapter, when you see the titles, you see the classic full-page story of a comic book represented in the opening titles. The four tales of mayhem or whatever they say in the titles, played out from start to end but they had an overlap. So it starts, the cold open with the robot couple coming home, and it ends with you seeing that repeated. There are some other crossovers where you saw the werewolf girls pull up in front of that house and they almost run into Rhonda, and then you realize, oh yeah that's the girls, I've already seen that story. So there were crossovers just at the end of the chapter. And like I say, we introduce the crossovers a little more frequently and changed the order of the stories.

-KTH: That aspect really makes ***Trick 'r Treat*** unique amongst horror anthology films. And I actually sometimes feel like labeling it as an anthology is kind of incorrect. I don't know if you've ever heard the term "hyperlink cinema," but it refers to films like ***Traffic***, ***Crash***, ***Magnolia***, ***Pulp Fiction***, ***Love Actually***, things like that. I wonder, did films like that ever come up in your discussions with Michael? Were there any films that came up when you were talking about structure?

-RI: I think we talked about maybe ***Pulp Fiction***. We said, oh yeah, ***Pulp Fiction*** does a good job of crossing over one tale to the next and sort of jumping time back and forth over the course of the evening and people are alive at the end who are dead in the middle. There's a reworking of audience expectations of who's loyalties you're rooting for. So we did talk about ***Pulp Fiction*** a little bit, just more the effect of it, you know? There were so many movie references within ***Trick 'r Treat*** that I think Mike was more interested in showcasing the in-jokes and the references... There were all kinds of little tributes to horror films along the way, and I think we paid more attention to those features...

-KTH: I find it really interesting that the structure of ***Trick 'r Treat*** seemed to have come very organically. I wonder if there are times, as an editor, where you're so involved in the story, and the story really changes shape drastically as you go, do you ever reach a point where you're wondering if the audience has everything they need to keep up with the story, and understand what's going on?

-RI: That's what test screenings are for. Certainly in the horror genre, just like in comedy, you're looking for an impact that's involuntary. You want people to jump, you want people to laugh. It's not a voluntary reaction, so you have to test those moments out. You can't rationalize them. You can't sit in the editing room and say, oh there's a laugh here. They may not. It's all about beats and timing in comedy and the same is true in horror. There are certain rhythms to a horror reveal that you have to either, just like the movie, you have to abide by the rules in an interesting and unobstructive way. And that's what the test screenings are for.

Ultimately that's how we came to modify the structure to feature those scary moments, those jump scares, those reveals in a pattern that was a little more evenly distributed than all of them happening at a certain point in the timeline of the movie. We did pay attention to where jump scares happen, where big reveals happen, where information was gained by the audience that they didn't necessarily know going in... We paid a lot of attention to laying those bread crumbs out and rearranging them... We certainly played around with structure and with like, how many times can we cut away from one story and go to the next? How can we interweave the stories more than we have? I think we probably ended up backing off on a couple transitions to other threads of the story. We were just forcing it too much.

Like you said, there are some naturally organic crossovers, and if we couldn't make those seem natural, like they were always in the design even though they weren't, then we didn't want them to be in the movie. We wanted to be true to the spirit of the movie which was that it was a multi-threaded narrative and we wanted to keep the audience more on its toes.

I think that was one of the things that we discovered with the first screening was that if you indicate to the audience that each chapter is its own standalone, then they grow to anticipate the end of each chapter just by their own internal clock. They know it's a 90 minute movie and every segment of it is going to be 23 minutes roughly, or whatever. When I was a kid going to horror movies I knew when the end of one segment was coming up; when it was going to be time. You can feel it in a story when it's wrapping up you feel like you're in act three.

One of the things I think we did successfully was defeat that internal clock to throw it out of rhythm. So suddenly you're back in the werewolf story and you're, oh we're picking up with the principal again. And we did that deliberately in a way that was more organic, crossing over sound effects or using the turn of a character as a reaction to something that was happening in another story.

-The takeaway: There's so much to unpack from what Robert had to say. I hope that you'll similarly be able to look at your film's structure more scrupulously after hearing about the process that ***Trick 'r Treat*** went through. Even the best filmmakers will discover late in the game that their script was not perfect, and that a better movie is still to be found in the editing room. I found this to be particularly helpful when I was editing my film,

Gravedigger Dave's Halfway House. Robert's story of how ***Trick 'r Treat*** went from the version in the script to the version we all know today inspired me to experiment with the ordering of my short films to find the pacing that would work best.

Editor William Szarka told me he went through a similar process with the 1986 anthology, ***Deadtime Stories***. I first met Bill in 2007, early in my career, and began freelancing for him on a variety of projects, the most well-known of which is ***The Untold Christmas Story***. This was a behind the scenes documentary about Bob Clark's holiday classic, ***A Christmas Story***, on which I logged and transcribed interviews. It was fairly tedious work, but I enjoyed helping Bill on that project and others. Years later, when I reached out to him about his work on ***Deadtime Stories***, he was happy to give me the inside scoop on the film. It was great reconnecting with him. Over the phone, he told me:

> So the story with ***Deadtime Stories*** was... Jeff [Delman, Director] had a rough cut and my boss had actually invested money in the movie. So he had to shoot a few more scenes. What they wanted me to do was basically come in and fine tune the footage already shot, cut the new stuff into the movie, and just finesse it because it needed pacing. It was kind of slow moving. I think what he tried to do - because it was short -

> some of the scenes were running long so he would have the length to make a full-length movie… Some of the stories, I remember the pacing wasn't the same… Jeff at that point was kind of burnt out. Because I know he had been working on the movie for maybe a couple of years. He had obviously put his own money into it. So at that point he kind of just stood back. I was fresh, so I started just doing stuff and he was liking it.

When editing ***Gravedigger Dave's Halfway House***, I realized it'd be a stretch to hit the obligatory 90 minutes with the footage I had shot. Instead of falling into the trap that Bill describes, I resigned to cut the longer-running scenes down. I wound up with a 72 minute film, and Bill's advice helped it get there. Thinking further about what both Robert Ivison and Bill said, I can't overstate the value of having an unbiased set of eyes evaluate the pacing of a film. Anthologies are difficult to pace because of their inherent stopping and starting in between stories. Getting feedback can give your film some much-needed perspective.

INTERVIEW WITH BRAD MISKA

(V/H/S & SOUTHBOUND PRODUCER)

-Background: Though Brad has produced some great films, he's probably best-known as the co-founder of the horror website, Bloody Disgusting. If you're unfamiliar, it's been a great source for horror movie news online since 2001, which means that Brad knows basically everything about the horror genre.

-Keith Tyler Hopkins: I want to ask you about the concept for the first ***V/H/S*** film. How did the idea come about?

-Brad Miska: Salient Media wanted to do films with Bloody Disgusting and they also had a TV department over there. I had originally pitched this as a TV series and I wanted to do a found footage-style ***Tales from the Crypt*** series about a bunch of kids who find videos and tapes and hidden government files. So it was a mix between ***X-Files*** and ***Tales from the Crypt***. The film department over there really wanted to do it as a film and then use that to pitch a TV series, which never came to fruition. It's always been a little frustrating because that's sort of how I intended it.

At the time, Simon Barret [***V/H/S*** writer/producer] and Adam Wingard [***V/H/S*** director], and I associate produced and got financed ***A Horrible Way to Die***, and we were looking to do another project with them. They had brought us ***You're Next***, and they ended up doing ***You're Next*** with Snoot Films... We had actually put in a bid and Snoot outbid us and they went and made that movie with Snoot. Adam and Simon, we were like, well let's do something else together. Then I had this idea for ***V/H/S*** and wanted Simon to write the pilot.

So Simon came in and wrote, and took my idea, then he put his own dirty spin on it. Grotesqued it up and put it in an old man's house. And they had some time, if I remember correctly, they had some time before they went to go shoot ***You're Next.*** They had like a small window. So Salient and the other producer at Salient, Gary Binkow [***V/H/S*** producer], they approved the financing for the wraparound. We just figured we'd make the movie as we go. So they ran off and they shot all their stuff, the wraparound, before ***You're Next***... So we had this raw footage and it gave us the vibe for the whole thing. We knew the ugliness of it and what we wanted it to look like and feel like... Then we just started going from filmmaker to filmmaker and piecemealing it together. That's how it started.

-KTH: When you went to the filmmakers to make the shorts that would go within the wraparound, what kind of mandates were there? Obviously, there was an aesthetic. Was there any story content that you knew had to be in the shorts?

-BM: The origin of ***V/H/S***, outside of the actual concept, is through Simon and me hanging out. He's been a longtime friend of mine. We used to go to film festivals together. I watched a ton of movies with him... One of the things that we always do on the filmmaking spectrum is we look at films that we don't like and address that. So as opposed to making a movie that's inspired by something, ***V/H/S*** isn't inspired by anything. There was nothing before it that we were like, oh I love this, let's do that. But it's inspired by things that we don't like.... I guess that comes from the critical side of me and the fact that I'm a film critic. I look at a lot of films and I see a lot of problems with them, things that I would do differently. So when we went into ***V/H/S*** the idea was, how can we do something better than the predecessors? It's not to insult any anthologies that came before us because there's fantastic anthologies before us. It's just, what could we do to evolve it, do something different?

So what are the mandates? We're sort of looking at the things we didn't like about found footage and not repeating that. So one mandate that I remember very specifically was to try not to end it with the dropped camera… We feel like we almost were at the tail end of the whole craze. So it's kind of a snark at all of those found footage movies where they open with: this is based on a true story. Or it ends with the camera drop and then it just goes to credits like it's real. So there's this moment in the first one where the camera drops, and it's easily one of my favorite moments ever being at a film festival. When the camera drops and the entire audience stands up at the Sundance premiere because they thought it was over. And that was like a fuck you. No, it's not over. That's not how these should end…

We knew from day one we were going to end it with a music video of sorts. We didn't know how we were going to do it, we just knew that we weren't trying to trick anybody. We weren't trying to say, hey this is real, you should believe it. What we were trying to say is we want to have fun. This should be a fun movie, and wild and crazy shit is gonna happen, and when it ends it's gonna be a music video. It's gonna look like it's been edited together by somebody... You don't want to discount ***Trick 'r Treat***'s organic interweaving of stories which was always exciting, and trying to find a way to have them connect even if they don't connect, just like with the tapes.

In terms of the look and feel of it, there was just a lot of discussion amongst all the filmmakers. Adam and Simon took the lead and made sure to have conversations with everyone about how they were going to shoot it, and how it was going to look, and making sure that it felt organic. Not everyone did it the same way but everyone was still able to give it the sort of ugly dirty look, which we deviate from on the third film, which maybe was a mistake.

But mostly I think it was a mistake because people misunderstood what we were trying to say about it. It's one of those things where you can't really talk to the audience. You can't say, hey guys you sort of misunderstood this. They take it as it is, and they took it at face value and didn't like it. And I'm totally fine with that. I think the things that we did were kinda cool. But we tried to be flashy and break more rules, because we were never staying in the lanes. We were always trying to do things that were sorta outside of the box. And that was the point of the third one too. To try and deviate from all the rules. And then everyone was like, look at all the rules they're breaking...

The only thing with the third one, we wanted it to be more polished and add more score type stuff to it. And people were like, it's found footage, that doesn't make any sense. Because people don't seem to understand that what they're watching is a mixtape. They're not watching the actual tape of the footage. Somebody made this tape and they're watching the tape that somebody made. So we were just like, let's really break loose with this and do polished shit and break timelines and stuff. It just didn't connect with people…

The second one was really easy because we learned from the mistakes of the first one and just kinda flowed right into the second one, and were able to assemble it really quickly… Everyone really wanted to be part of it. So it was a phone call and everyone was just like, sure.

-KTH: As far as budgeting goes, is it the kind of thing where the producers of the short have to supply their own budget and then on the backend of the release of the feature maybe they get a little bit? Or you guys, as the producers of the feature, supply a certain amount of money to the folks making the short? How does that work?

-BM: I don't like wasting people's time. So the first thing we asked them to do was to just submit log lines. And if we were into any of the log lines, we were like, alright, let's roll with this one... So we got tons of different filmmakers pitching stuff. Some really really cool ideas. The problem was they either got it or they didn't.

So when you're talking about doing something like ***V/H/S*** we really wanted to make sure the filmmakers understood the specific vibe we were coming from. It was a bummer because there were a lot of really cool filmmakers that we had lined up for the second one and there's only so many slots. You kinda have to zero in on who feels right; feels like they get it.

So they pitched a one-pager. Then if we liked the one-pager what they would do is they would write out their full script. And then they would submit their budget for approval, and once the budget got approved they'd set up their own company and the funds would be transferred to that company. And then they would go shoot their short and then we would acquire the short from that company....

It's a little difficult when you're dealing with unions and stuff. You have to abide by the budgetary constraints and stuff like that. But making short films and assembling them is sort of a different thing...

That's actually one of the problems with making an anthology film is there's not a lot of meat on the bone. You're talking a lot of filmmakers, a lot of producers. There's not a lot of meat on the bone. It gets spread really thin. So a lot of these people were doing it for the love of the genre, and doing something fun with friends, and that kind of thing. Not to make a gazillion dollars or anything like that.

-KTH: A criticism I often read of anthology films, critics will say that they're unevenly paced. But I think fans of this particular subgenre accept that as being inherent to genre. There's a lot of starting and stopping and starting and stopping in anthology films. I just wanted your take on the uneven pacing that's kind of in all of these movies.

-BM: There's several different things that go with that. I don't think an anthology film should be unevenly paced and I think a lot of that reflects on the budget and the financiers... Anthologies you're just kinda like, it drags along for months and months and months. It's not that easy to go, hey this all works except for this. Can we have another thirty thousand dollars to go back and shoot something else? And it's like, well what'll we do with that one? Throw it in the garbage? That seems insane. That's money in the garbage. So oftentimes you see an anthology and you go, eh, some of it was good and then some of it was really bad. And that's just because that's the product of what they locked themselves into...

With something like ***Southbound*** we played with fire in the sense that we could not tailor it. ***V/H/S,*** we were able to tweak stuff and watch them and put them in different orders and we could play with it. We couldn't do that with ***Southbound***. We knew exactly where everything was going. And if something didn't work we were locked into it. And there was nothing we could do about it. But the thing that gets me though, when you see a really long anthology or something, and there's a bunch of bad stuff. That's just them not wanting to be bad guys and cut people out. Looking at ***V/H/S*** we probably could've trimmed that down. We probably could've maybe even cut a segment or whatnot. But we were kinda just committed to rolling with what we had and how we had it. The unevenness, it's sort of a hard thing to balance...

When you go in and make a movie, 99.9 % of the time you are presenting a project fully ready to go. So a lot of these people, like ***Holidays*** or whatever. They go in, they have the filmmakers, they have the scripts. They go, here are the filmmakers, here's the script, here's the budget. They get the money, they go, they shoot, it's done, and that's it. When we made ***V/H/S*** and ***V/H/S 2*** it was not like that. It was, we have the money, now let's do whatever the fuck we want and do something cool. So we were able to sort of play with it and do it in a very unorthodox way, and I think it reflects that on screen.

A lot of other filmmakers just don't have that luxury and that's why I think a lot of them end up being very uneven. Or they just work with bad filmmakers because they just are friends with them and it's all they could get... There's some I do not like, and a lot of the reason I don't like some of these is because you can tell that they just head for the stupid concept and then threw a bunch of filmmakers together and then figured it would just work. And that's not how you make an anthology. You can't just pluck four random filmmakers out of the sky and say, hey you guys, get in a room and make a movie together. That's insane thinking. And you can see it on the screen with a lot of these movies. And then when you have something like ***Southbound*** where you pick a bunch of similar filmmakers who are all friends with each other, and all respect each other, and can sit there and work together... you get something that feels a lot more coherent. So ***Southbound*** should feel like a singular movie. If somebody said one filmmaker made it then maybe you would believe that, because everyone was working together.

-KTH: The first time I watched ***Southbound*** I went into it knowing it was an anthology. When I was a kid we'd sit around the campfire and someone would start a ghost story and then midway through they'd stop and it would get passed to the next person. That person would continue and then they'd stop and it would get passed to the next person, and so on. The first time I watched ***Southbound***, I was like, holy crap, this is the filmmaking version of that.

-BM: That really is exactly how that was put together. So it started with, I had an idea. Radio Silence [***Southbound*** segment directors] totally changed it into their own idea, so I can't take credit for that. Their concept was a loop. They came in with their pitch. Roxanne [Benjamin, ***Southbound*** segment director] had talked to me about directing and she went with Susan Burke [***Southbound*** segment writer] and wrote hers... So those two were written, and then I wanna say Patrick [Hovarth, ***Southbound*** segment director] came in later. He was a little later and was able to sort of reflect on what stories were being told. He felt like it needed a mythology. So it is kinda what you're saying. He had a story to the mythology and had information. And then Bruckner [David, ***Southbound*** segment director] had a story originally and then stepped back and looked at everything and was like, nah, this doesn't work in the storytelling model. If I change it to something more like this then it fits and we get a better narrative. So like you're saying, it was kind of like a passing of the story. And then everyone worked together to talk about transitions and how they can transition it and what it would look like and that kind of stuff. It was a really really cool experience.

-KTH: In many anthology films you can tell that there's these crews that are kind of working in total isolation from one another. You can often even tell, like, this one was clearly made with a different camera than that one. But there's this cohesion in ***Southbound*** that it really feels like a feature where everyone was on the set at the same time. Is that how ***Southbound*** was made?

-BM: Kind of sort of. With all of the other anthologies that I've made, everyone gets their money and goes and does their own thing. This was the first one where we had it lined up so it was the same crew, just different actors popping in, different directors popping in. That actually caused a problem with the union, who changed our classification. So basically all of our contingency money got used up before we were even on set. So we had to have a conversation where it was like, nobody can fuck up! There was literally no money if there's a fuck up, so nobody can go over. Nothing can be fucked up. And everyone was like, that doesn't happen, ever. So we kinda went in terrified. Absolutely terrified.

Patrick shot first and Patrick, man, talk about the kind of director who sets the tone. I think that's a good lesson to be learned is, a happy crew can make a big difference on your production. And he really set the tone. Just a really fun, nice guy. Positive reinforcer. The crew just absolutely loved him and it got everyone rolling on the right track. Once he finished, I think Roxanne was on all the sets with me. I was on Patrick's and then Roxanne shot second. I was only on her set for a day. But everyone visited everyone's set and was kind of hanging out. Cause it was just a few hour drive from Los Angeles. Everyone kinda knew what was going on... But it was the same crew, so it was the same makeup department, same set dressers. The only difference was they had different DPs and their own ADs and stuff like that... A lot of that credit goes to Chris Harding [***Southbound*** producer]. He's with Snoot [Entertainment] and he helped assemble a lot of that stuff and it made a huge difference having that cohesion. You can also run into a problem with that too, because if you have a bad crew then the whole movie is shit and there's nothing you can do about it.

-KTH: You said before that ***V/H/S*** is kinda like a mixtape. With ***Southbound*** you can really feel- not to make a pun- but you can feel that there's a roadmap there, and that everyone's following the same map.

-BM: And it's funny too, 'cause the movie is kinda the anti-***V/H/S***, because we made ***V/H/S*** and then we made ***V/H/S 2***, and then everyone started copying us. Like I was telling you earlier, when we made ***V/H/S***, the whole point of ***V/H/S*** was a response to things we didn't like in the subgenre. We were trying to do something different and then here comes all these movies just copying us. So there was a ton of these weird tape movies that were coming out, these indie tape movies, and a bunch of anthologies that were coming out very similarly structured. And we were sitting here just going, what the fuck? Can you do something different? Try something fucking different. You've really got to do the same fucking thing? Seriously? So ***Southbound*** was our response, once again, to everybody doing something we don't like... So let's flip the script all over again and let's try and make something that's insanely cohesive and stunning and has huge scope and feels like you can breathe, versus super claustrophobic, and I think we pulled it off with that. It was kinda crazy that we were able to do that twice.

-KTH: For emerging filmmakers, or people who perhaps want to get into filmmaking, is there power in collaborating with other directors and releasing an anthology as a team? Does it help in distribution? Does it help in pooling budgets, pooling creativity, and getting something that's feature-length out into the world?

-BM: Names always help, and it's always sort of a difficult thing, 'cause you go in and you tell these people with money, hey I really wanna make this thing. And they go, well who's doing it? Like, just trust me, we're getting the right people to make the right movie... For aspiring filmmakers obviously having names is important to help get money and to sell it, but at the same time you might have to sacrifice some creativity with that, or continuity. Anthologies aren't easy... There's a lot of things that go into making it feel right. You're not making a short film festival. You're trying to make a movie.

INTERVIEW WITH SIMON BARRETT

(ABCs OF DEATH & V/H/S WRITER)

-Background: As a segment writer on both ***V/H/S*** and ***The ABCs of Death***, I knew Simon would be a great person to interview for the book. Simon collaborates frequently with Adam Wingard, their first claim to fame being the slasher film, ***You're Next***.

-Keith Tyler Hopkins: ***V/H/S*** and ***ABCs***, both of those films came out the same year, but I was wondering which one you worked on first,

-Simon Barrett: The funny thing is they did happen a bit simultaneously, but I did work on ***V/H/S*** first... The interesting thing about ***V/H/S*** is Adam Wingard and I filmed the wraparound before any other segments were shot. And we shot it in my hometown of Columbia, Missouri while we were in pre-production for the film, ***You're Next***. We'd done the movie ***A Horrible Way to Die*** with Brad Miska [Producer of ***V/H/S*** and ***Southbound***], which we'd filmed in early 2010. And it premiered at Toronto in September of 2010. Around then was the time that Brad started pitching his concept for ***V/H/S*** to us…

And the name, ***V/H/S***, came from our other producer, Roxanne Benjamin. It was just called, "The Bloody Disgusting Horror Anthology," or whatever. And the notion was that it was going to be a web series at first. Just a series of short films with an overarching mythology of each of the films being found footage horror. And you'd have this kind of loose throughline on the series, which is people finding these cursed tapes. But we really didn't have any more than that. I actually ended up talking to Brad and Adam specifically about how if we conceived it as a feature film anthology I knew we could make it. I didn't know what the marketing was for a TV series or web series, but if we limited the scope and limited the budget then I knew it was at least something that we could finish.

And again, the idea at the time was that this was just something we'd create for Bloody Disgusting who had their own video label and were releasing films… It was going to be their first in-house title and maybe come out through them, or maybe the shorts would come out on their website. We hadn't really figured it out… I wanted to do an old school, and when I say "old school" I mean a more traditional, anthology than what I'd seen recently. Meaning, going back to the Amicus ***Tales from the Crypt*** films, ***Vault of Horror***, ***Asylum***, certain things like that being among my personal favorite anthologies. And I hadn't really seen a film do anything like that since Rusty Cundieff's ***Tales from the Hood***…

Since then all the anthology films I'd seen had been ***Three***, ***Three 2***, ***Phobia***… and all those films were different segments by different directors. They were just kind of lumped together and there was no real throughline or stylistic unity. We knew we were going to do the same type of model essentially: each individual filmmaker would cut their segments themselves, shoot it with their own crew, have total freedom. But we were concerned about, how does this feel like a complete film and not just like watching a handful of shorts? And I think that's why Brad's original idea of doing it found footage, focusing on the actual finding of the footage as the core premise was quite brilliant. More brilliant than I think any of us realized at the time because by forcing us all to do found footage, we embraced the notion of doing found footage truly in a raw, almost shitty, way that you couldn't get away with on a Hollywood film. It created that stylistic consistency and coherency that I personally felt was lacking from the anthology films that I had seen.

To this day when I watch a lot of anthologies that I think were maybe inspired by ***V/H/S*** and ***ABCs of Death***, and that model of asking a bunch of filmmakers to make extremely low-budget short films that can be assembled into a marketable feature, the main thing that bothers me about them is the complete inconsistency between how they're shot, and how they're paced, and so on. But by limiting us to shooting found footage in a fairly real way... it was a real fun creative challenge.

If you watch ***V/H/S*** carefully, you can tell that when Adam and I filmed the wraparound we didn't know how many segments there were going to be. That's why there's a lot of footage of people putting tapes in a VCR and looking at it. It's because we didn't know if there was going to be three segments or five segments... So we were just trying to shoot a bunch of footage that would work. But what we were also trying to do was establish- for all of the other filmmakers that were going to come on to this project- this is the style, this is the tone. So we were filming it with a VHS camera that I had got for my 13th birthday... So it really looked awful. And when we started showing it to filmmakers… that actually really excited all those guys. They saw how oddly unprofessional what Adam and I were doing was, and were like, that's interesting, that's different.

At the time found footage itself had become such a phenomenon after the release of ***The Last Exorcism*** and ***Paranormal Activity***, but a lot of the found footage films were very glossy, very overproduced. They were all shot on 35mm lenses and then degraded in post to give them a certain ugly video look. And we were like, skip that. Let's actually shoot this on the lowest tier of consumer video. The wraparound ended up being what everyone looked to to be like, okay how do we do this and how do we take this further?

But we were really flying quite blind. I wrote a script and then Adam and I basically threw it out... But then we hired our actors... people who were very adept at improv and so we were able to make everything feel spontaneous. And we were actually trespassing. We didn't have permits to film, because Columbia, Missouri doesn't have filming permits. So we were getting the police called on us and we were really doing it very low-budget, very indie filmmaking style, which we were familiar with from doing other cheap movies.

So that was the inception of the ***V/H/S*** wraparound. The funny thing, it became a thing people thought we put a lot more thought into than we had… Then when the movie got into Sundance, we were like, oh jeez. I remember we were incredibly gratified, but it was also like, oh boy, this is going to make some people angry. And it certainly did.

-KTH: Moving on to ***ABCs of Death***, when you were approached about that film were you asked to pick a letter or were you assigned a letter? Did you know anything about what the other filmmakers were doing? Did you have to submit your script for approval? Or was it just, here's your letter, it's "Q," do whatever the heck you want.

-SB: Adam had a long term friendship with Ant Timpson [***The ABCs of Death*** producer]... Ant reached out to Adam, and I wasn't a part of that conversation, but he was assigned the letter, "Q." Honestly, I think the main reason for that, and Adam and I make jokes about this in our segment, was that we just were the smallest filmmakers in the anthology at the time, because we hadn't made ***You're Next***, and nobody knew who we were… We were the smaller, cheaper, filmmakers to pad out the film so we got a lousy letter [laughs]. We did think it was funny that we had gotten this terrible letter that didn't have that many words attached to it and made that the joke…

We knew that we were two-thirds of the way through the film, so we knew that we just had to be funny and quick. Because at two-thirds of the way… we were doing the math and people had already watched so many of these segments. We're not going to top anyone else in terms of gore, or being disturbing, or being scary. Our best option, given our personalities, was to just do something funny and just get out. And that was what we did and we got good reviews from it. It ended up being a very well-received segment… But once I did write that script, I think we did run it by Ant and Tim League [***ABCs*** producer]... Ant and Tim League were the only ones who read that draft and signed off on it…

In answer to the last thing you asked, yes filmmakers were talking to each other but we didn't really know very many people involved at the time. Again, this was at a point in Adam's and my career where we were both very isolated. We didn't know a lot of other filmmakers. We were just doing our own thing and we weren't doing it very successfully. Both of us had day jobs that were making us miserable and trying to make things work. ***You're Next*** hadn't premiered yet, and that was really the film that started our careers in a meaningful way.

-KTH: So did they send each group a little bit of a budget so that you guys weren't sinking too much of your own money into it?

-SB: We were sent $5,000. We ended up honestly spending about $7,000... We were still pretty broke, but we wanted to make sure we were actually paying our crew.... Certain things on our ***ABCs of Death*** shoot would've felt like luxuries on some of our earlier projects, including the ***V/H/S*** wraparound but because we were feeling a little more confident we were comfortable spending two grand… We spent a little more than we had to to try to make ourselves look good, which was the fun of ***ABCs of Death*** because it really was a competition between the filmmakers. It was an opportunity for a lesser-known filmmaker to make themselves look good to some of the better-known filmmakers.

INTERVIEW WITH ANT TIMPSON

(ABCs OF DEATH PRODUCER)

-Background: This interview is concise, but not without its useful nuggets of information. As one of the producers overseeing the compilation of all the short films used in the three ***ABCs*** films, Ant gives a bird's-eye view of the process.

-Keith Tyler Hopkins: The first two ***ABCs*** films credit you with "based on a nightmare by" and "based on a franchise dream by." Can you explain? Did the concept actually come to you in a dream or is it meant as a joke?

-Ant Timpson: Joke based on some truth. I did wake up with the ***ABCs*** idea after reading various ABC books to my children and sent a one-pager to my friend Tim League. The rest they say is infamy.

-KTH: Did you reach out to filmmakers to make shorts for the first ***ABCs*** film or was there a submission process?

-AT: Primarily we pinged filmmakers we had existing relationships with. The rest were filmmakers who reached out once they knew about the project.

-KTH: When a filmmaker gets a short into an ***ABCs*** movie, do they sign their rights away for the short to be used exclusively in the anthology, or is there a nonexclusive contract that you offer?

-AT: The content was created exclusively for the feature film, so the production entity owned the material. For the 26th submission in each ***ABCs*** feature we had a global contest and narrowed it down through public vote and finally the filmmakers themselves.

-KTH: What makes a great horror short? What are you looking for in an ***ABCs*** submission?

-AT: A strong beginning, middle and end. It's like that old "is it pornography?" query. The answer is always, I know it when I see it. For the submissions we were looking for originality along with assured direction.

-KTH: I haven't seen ***The Field Guide to Evil*** yet, but were you interested in doing a film that was different from the ***ABCs*** franchise in some way?

-AT: Definitely wanted to do something with global folklore for a long time and wanted to focus the content. If ***ABCs*** was an old circus, ***The Field Guide to Evil*** is like the Alligator Man exhibit.

INTERVIEW WITH MARIA OLSEN

(SOUTHBOUND ACTRESS)

-Background: As one who works in front of the camera, Maria offers a perspective that new filmmakers often overlook during production. Maria has a lot of insight on the value of acting in shorts and anthologies. And as this is a book about transitioning from short film to short film, it's especially fitting that Maria's character serves as the segue device between two segments in ***Southbound***.

-Keith Tyler Hopkins: You've acted in a lot of great productions, from small indie films, to bigger studio pictures. As a professional actor, can you talk about the benefits of doing a short film in comparison to a feature?

-Maria Olsen: A short film definitely means a shorter time commitment, and, these days, with the popularity of the anthology film on the rise, there's an increasing chance that the film will live on to be seen by the general public as part of a feature. Undoubtedly features are the name of the game in the indie film world, so getting your name on a feature because you shot a short that required minimum commitment of time and energy is definitely a prize!

-KTH: As an actor, you have to interpret the vision of the director, and on an anthology there can be a lot of directors steering the picture. Can you talk about what it's like working on a movie like this?

-MO: Whenever I've worked on features with multiple directors - and these include the single-story ***Starry Eyes*** and ***Paranormal Activity 3*** - the multiple directors have worked together in perfect harmony (at least from what I've seen!). With regard to the anthologies, and if we look at ***Southbound*** as an example, both David Bruckner and Patrick Horvath (the directors of my two segments) were in total agreement about how my character was to be portrayed, and there was never one moment of disagreement or confusion. They had extremely different directing styles, but this didn't stop them even for one moment from working together for the good of the film.

-KTH: In ***Southbound***, you played a character who appears in two segments, and is used to transition between those two segments. What was that production like?

-MO: ***Southbound*** was a production of contrasts for me. On the one hand, it reunited me with the amazing Patrick Horvath, who I had previously worked with on the award winning feature ***Die-Ner (Get It?)***. Patrick is an absolute joy to work with, and I constantly miss his sense of humor and infectious laugh, and being directed by him was like meeting up with an old friend. David Bruckner, on the other hand, was an unknown quantity when I first started on the film. I came to know him as an extremely meticulous and detail-oriented director who left no stone unturned in his quest to mould his actors into his vision of the story. He truly stretched me as a performer, and I look forward to working with him again because I know he will push me to the limit and beyond instead of letting me stay in my comfort zone.

-KTH: Is the experience different when you're working on a film that has one director, and thus a singular vision?

-MO: Yes, the experience is a little different, although, with anthologies, the different directors concentrate only on their own segments. With single-story features with multiple directors, the directors decide on a division of duties before shooting starts so that they each work to their strengths and that there is no confusion on set. For ***Starry Eyes***, for instance, Dennis and Kevin have said that they identified their own strengths early in the game and easily fell into the habit of accepting different groups of directorial responsibilities once on set.

-KTH: For aspiring actors, what is the value of working in short films that may end up in anthologies? From my perspective, it seems like it's a low time commitment, but still gets your name in a feature film, and that has value to someone building their career. What's your take?

-MO: If you're an aspiring actor, you should work on short films even if they DON'T end up in anthologies! Any opportunity to work on set should be grabbed with both hands as every project that a newbie actor works on gives them more and more confidence in themselves and helps them cope with that big break role when it finally comes. It's even more attractive for them when the short DOES appear in an anthology, because then they have a feature film under their belt!

-KTH: What are some things directors seem to not understand about your craft?

-MO: The issue that comes up most often is making actors hold a specific emotion for a length of time in order to change lighting etc. Unless you're an actor yourself, you don't really know the effort, concentration and focus it takes for an actor to stay in, for instance, an emotional state where he or she is crying/extremely angry/extremely sad etc. Physical discomfort is another thing an actor experiences that may not be glaringly obvious to the director and crew. Just last night I was lying on the freezing ground in the woods wearing only a nightdress and covered in blood that was getting colder by the second. The crew were dressed in whatever keeps them warm outdoors in the woods at night. And, while I am NOT saying THIS crew wasn't sympathetic to what I was going through, you can often find someone going about their job slowly, or even perhaps wasting time, while an actor is literally freezing or struggling to maintain a specific emotional state. A little awareness of what the actor is going through would go a long way.

INTERVIEW WITH ROBERTA SOLOMON

(CREMATIA MORTEM HOST)

-Background: I got to know Roberta while working in the marketing department for an NBC news affiliate. She was our station voice and I'd pester her weekly for voiceovers to use in our promotional spots. While you'd never know from chatting with her, Roberta is a pretty big deal. She's been the voice of an *Expendables* trailer, the Promax Virtual Experience, and TV stations across the country. Imagine my surprise when I learned that she also has led a double-life as renowned horror host, Crematia Mortem.

-Keith Tyler Hopkins: Can you briefly describe how you came to host horror films as Crematia Mortem?

-Roberta Solomon: I was working as the evening announcer on a Soft Rock radio station in Kansas City, when I became friends with the Creative Services Director from KSHB-TV. He'd visit his pals at the radio station from time to time. KSHB had been airing a show called "All Night Live" for some time. From 10pm until about 1am, they played old sitcoms and westerns and ***The Twilight Zone***, and featured a movie each night...

The show became so popular that KSHB decided to expand it to Saturday nights. But Ed [Muscare, host] didn't want to host the show six nights a week, so KSHB announced they were going to hold auditions for a Saturday night host...

One of the characters I created was this Country Western singer named Minnie, modeled vaguely after Dolly Parton… I could hear the TV crew laughing in the booth, and I was absolutely mortified because I thought I'd just made a complete fool out of myself. The next day, they called to tell me I got the job.

I hosted "All Night Live" on Saturday using the name Sally Roberts. I appeared on the show as several characters, including a roller derby queen named Wheels Butcherelli, my own mother and Minnie. We played episodes of *Tarzan*, some sitcoms, and a monster movie each week. After about 8 months, the director called me into her office and said, "We like the comedy bits you're doing, but they don't have anything to do with the movies we're showing. We'd like to retool the show and turn it into a 'Creature Feature.' Would you like to create a new character to host the show?"

I said yes, and decided immediately to call her Crematia. I bought a long black wig at a surplus store and a corset from Frederick's of Hollywood, went to garage sales and thrift stores and found some furniture and decor for the set, and Crematia was born. On my last night hosting "All Night Live" as Sally Roberts, I told the audience "My time as your host has come to an end. I've been let go, and next week you'll have a new host. I have no idea who she is…I guess they just dug her up somewhere." Crematia and the

"Creature Feature" debuted the following week, and the show ran for the next 8 years.

-KTH: You're part of a great tradition of TV horror hosts that began with **Vampira**. Can you talk about what it's been like to carry the torch?

-RS: Well, it's been surprising and delightful. When I started hosting the "Creature Feature" as Crematia, of course I wanted to honor the tradition I'd grown up with, which included Morticia Addams, Lily Munster. I'd seen photos of **Vampira** and was transfixed as a kid. I definitely modeled Crematia after them: I wanted her to be loving and slightly out of touch; funny, creepy, beautiful, and kid-friendly! The thing that's the most humbling and wonderful is that so many people remember Crematia with such fondness, 30+ years after the show ended, and that they include her in the horror host pantheon! There's not a week that goes by without somebody reaching out to ask about Crematia, and to tell me what a great part of their childhood she was. And there are some new projects in the works by other performers who were inspired by Crematia, so the horror host torch is being passed.

-KTH: Why do you think puns, levity and humor pair so well with horror films?

-RS: Well, it's “whistling in the graveyard,” right? For most of the films we played, the jokes just kinda wrote themselves! For my own part, I knew that there were lots of kids watching, and I wanted them not to be afraid of the Creature Features they were seeing. Rather than pointing out the scary parts, I wanted them to feel safe watching them! So jokes about the monsters became a way of making them less scary for the kids. And of course, since Crematia's premise was that she'd been hanging around in a coffin for a looooong time, she was always slightly out of touch with reality. Her misunderstanding things was the basis for a lot of humor.

-KTH: What are the key ingredients to creating a memorable horror host?

-RS: Create a backstory for your character. Where did you come from? How did you turn out the way you did? What's your relationship to the other characters who join you on the show? Honor the horror host tradition but create your own monster "brand." It's not about YOU. It's about the people who are watching your show. Everything you do should be for them. It helps to know someone who's an undertaker. (Crematia's coffin came from the undertaker at the Federal Penitentiary at Leavenworth.)

-The takeaway: One of the greatest horror hosts in the history of anthology TV is HBO’s Cryptkeeper. In the documentary, ***Tales from the Crypt: From Comic Books to Television***, Jack Wohl (President of Tales from the Crypt Productions) says, "The key to the Cryptkeeper is that he's comedy relief. He sometimes can get a little ghoulish, but never really over the top. He's there to ease the pain of being scared, perhaps."

Combine Jack's sentiments with Roberta's great advice and you're well on your way to crafting a memorable horror host for your anthology.

INTERVIEW WITH RON OLIVER

(ARE YOU AFRAID OF THE DARK? & GOOSEBUMPS DIRECTOR)

-Background: I did reach out to R.L. Stine for an interview, and even though he declined, I was flattered that he responded at all. Instead of giving up, I started digging and stumbled upon Ron's filmography. When I saw that he had helmed 17 episodes of ***Are You Afraid of the Dark?*** and 16 episodes of ***Goosebumps*** I knew I had to get his insight. He worked closely with both Stine and ***AYAOTD?*** creator D.J. McHale, and has a wealth of knowledge about working on ongoing anthology series.

-Keith Tyler Hopkins: How did you get involved in directing for ***Are You Afraid of the Dark?***

-Ron Oliver: My second movie - my first as a director - was a horror comedy called ***Prom Night Three: The Last Kiss***. The creator/producer of ***AYAOTD?*** - D.J. MacHale - had seen the movie and asked me to have lunch with him in L.A. to discuss doing the first episode of the series - "The Tale of the Phantom Cab." I read the script, loved it, and said yes. About three days into the filming of that episode, the network and D.J. asked me to stay up in Montreal awhile longer and do more episodes - so I ended up staying there for a couple of months and directed four episodes in a row. And then the network [Nickelodeon] asked me to go to London England to do ***The Tomorrow People*** for them, so I had to leave ***Dark*** for a while…but I came back for season two, and all the rest...

-KTH: When directing an episode of this show, were there certain mandates you had to follow? I mean in terms of tone, content, outcome for the protagonist, etc.

-RO: As it was an anthology show, we (directors) were pretty free to make up our own worlds with each episode. Obviously we followed the script in terms of the story beats and so forth, but the tone of the episodes were usually set during a "tone meeting" between director/producer/writer to make sure we were all on the same page. Only once did I go off the rails a bit with an episode I wrote called "The Tale of the Full Moon," which was very stylized - sort of a John Waters/Joe Dante version of the show. I remember getting some pushback from the network as they thought it was too "campy" (which is usually a code word for "too gay" lol!) but then when the show was done, complete with big band soundtrack, everybody loved it.

-KTH: Was there any sort of style guide for directors to make sure each episode felt like the others in the series?

-RO: Not really. The great thing about ***Dark*** - and D.J. MacHale - was that they gave us a great deal of creative freedom to bring our own sensibility to the shows. As long as they were fun, scary and looked good, we were okay.

-KTH: As far as the wraparounds at the campfire, did each director shoot their own scenes for their episode, or were all of the Midnight Society scenes shot by a second unit to be inserted when needed?

-RO: D.J. MacHale directed most of those I believe - although there may have been a guest director or two at some point, I forget. I wasn't around for those, they were generally block shot over a week or two, in the studio.

-KTH: ***AYAOTD?*** was the first anthology horror TV series I ever watched, and I know I'm not alone. Was there ever any discussion during production about how the series could be an entire generation's entry point to the horror genre?

-RO: Absolutely! I remember having a production meeting one day and we were trying to find a shortcut for something, and I said something like "remember the shows WE watched as kids? Well, it might not seem like it at the time - as we rush around trying to shoot these kid shows on budget and on schedule - but this stuff will be what the next generation of US remembers! So we have a real responsibility to make these shows as high quality and enjoyable as we can." I think I did the same speech during ***Goosebumps***, too.

We were always aware that what we were doing was going to have an impact on the audience at the time - but I don't think any of us really believed these shows would be remembered and talked about over 25 years later! I often meet crew members on my current films and they are so wonderful telling me how much ***Dark*** and ***Goosebumps*** had meant to them as kids - and how so many got into film or tv because of inspiration from those shows. Kinda makes you feel a bit proud….!

-KTH: Having gone from ***AYAOTD?*** to ***Goosebumps***, are there different challenges when adapting a book series as opposed to directing an original script?

-RO: Not particularly. The script is the script - whether it comes from an original idea or a book. I adapted I think maybe a dozen of RL Stine's books for the tv show - and another couple for movies - and the challenge there has always been that Bob's books are aimed at a certain age level of reader, and a lot of that doesn't translate well to film. But there's always a great central concept or idea or two in the book that you can take and extrapolate into a full screenplay.

-KTH: During production, how important was it that each episode stay true to its source material?

-RO: Do you mean script or book? In either case, we would have script approvals come from the network - either Nickelodeon or Fox Kids TV - and we were obliged to stick to the script as much as possible. Sometimes we'd improvise dialogue or a bit of business and try to get it past the network - sometimes it would fly and sometimes we'd get the dreaded "network notes!" But usually the scripts were so well constructed that we could just let them come to life on the soundstage and it would work out fine.

-KTH: On shows like these, how do you wind up directing certain episodes and not others? Did you pitch concepts for books that you connected with, or were episodes simply assigned to certain directors?

-RO: Usually I'd end up directing the episodes I wrote, and then occasionally somebody else would write a script or have a story idea that I loved and I'd campaign to do that one. On ***Dark*** I got a lot of the shows involving CLOWNS because D.J. HATED CLOWNS and was scared of them, so I got the really creepy stories! When it came to ***Goosebumps***, the producers would select the books they wanted to adapt and either give me a choice of them or ask me to direct a script already in place.

-KTH: Do you have favorite episodes from either show?

-RO: YES! On ***Are You Afraid of the Dark?*** I loved two episodes for different reasons: "The Tale of the Full Moon" was the first time that, as a writer/director, I felt that I had actually "nailed it" in terms of story, tone, character and theme - and underlying message. It's the story of a family with a rather unusual relative and how that becomes a metaphor for diversity and acceptance; and how love conquers all.

"The Tale of Station 109.1" was special because it's where I met one of my dearest friends, the actor Ryan Gosling; it was his first dramatic role (at 14) and we bonded instantly on that episode. I worked with him whenever we could (including ***Goosebumps***!) and have stayed friends for the past twenty years - he was actually my Best Man. He's turned into a wonderful actor, obviously, but I'm more proud of the man he's become - he's a terrific husband to Eva and a great dad to his kids.

As for ***Goosebumps*** - I guess my absolute favorite episode would be the final one, a two parter called "Cry of the Cat." It was a meta-episode I wrote based on the book; but instead of following the book's plot, I made it into a faux-"behind the scenes" story which then became a full on horror story as we progressed. The opening scene - a parody of ***The Exorcist*** - is amongst my most favorite directing and writing in my entire career.

I remember submitting the script to Bob and Jane Stine - they both read it and called me and said "you're either crazy or a genius and we love it!" So having that kind of blessing meant a lot, but also we all kind of knew that this was going to be the last ***Goosebumps*** episode, so doing a bit of a send up of all the years of making the show was fun too!

As for fond memories — I learned so much from the creative people on both of those series - ***Dark*** was my first episodic series, as I'd only made three features up until then - two horror and a thriller - so I was still finding my way and my own visual sensibility. But the team we had in Montreal for ***Dark*** and the creatives in Toronto for ***Goosebumps*** were so supportive and encouraging, it really taught me a great deal about storytelling - and about dealing with large groups of artists!

Plus being in Montreal every summer for several years was kind of amazing too - such a beautiful city with such wonderful people, great music, great food - it was a marvelous experience all around!

INTERVIEW WITH BEDE BLAKE

(CREEPED OUT CO-CREATOR)

-Background: It was kind of an adventure getting in touch with Bede. I reached out to BBC and got a hold of Katie, who passed me on to Jo, who sent me to Lidia, who asked that I send her my questions for Bede. I was caught off guard and had to write up my questions for him really quick. To my surprise, Lidia responded the next day with Bede's email address, writing that he was happy to do the interview.

-Keith Tyler Hopkins: Being a child of the 90s, ***Creeped Out*** reminds me of the horror shows I used to watch, like ***Are You Afraid of the Dark?*** and ***Goosebumps***. Was there a conscious effort on your part to continue in the vein of kids anthology shows like this?

-Bede Blake: Oh man, absolutely. In fact that's where the conversation started - whilst talking about other 'regular' ideas to pitch, one of us said: "What I'd really love to do is…" Along with ***Are You Afraid Of The Dark?*** and ***Goosebumps*** there is a long history of dozens of weird and spooky anthology shows including ***Twilight Zone*** and ***Amazing Stories***, which we were exposed to growing up, all of which were big influences in different ways. Something that you're conscious of as writers is that what made you fall in love with screenwriting in the first place was TV shows and movies you saw as a kid. That's where it all starts. So when you come to write for a new generation of kids, you find yourself wanting to create the same kinds of wonder you experienced - and hopefully create a few new writers along the way too.

-KTH: I think The Curious is a captivating character. Can you tell me how the idea for him came about?

-BB: Like the shows mentioned above, we always wanted an introduction and sign-off for each little standalone 'mini-movie', as we call them. But, as with the stories themselves, we didn't want too much explained and also to maintain a real sense of mystery. The kind where you start to fill in the blanks yourself. That's where the mask came from. Even though we have some ideas about who or what The Curious is, we want the character to be unknowable. That creates a sense of fear and a sense of imagination - the two states we want to put the audience in with our stories.

-KTH: Why was it important to have The Curious linking each episode, as opposed to the approach taken on shows like ***Black Mirror***, in which theme and subject matter are the primary things linking each episode?

-BB: To our eternal surprise, anthology shows are now everywhere, but believe it or not, this show took such a long road to get made, that when we originally pitched it, anthologies were non-existent on contemporary TV. We were trying to revive an old format. Our original pitch even predates ***Stranger Things***. God bless them but broadcasters tend to freak out when you tell them there are no continuing characters for the audience to bond with episode in and episode out. At least they did back then. The Curious was one way of solving that problem - giving the audience a recognisable face that told them they were home each episode. It's just ironic that you don't see his face.

-KTH: The Curious is a very versatile character, storytelling wise. The way he's written allows for many different types of stories in many different places. How important is it to the creative longevity of the show that he remains open ended?

-BB: I think the moment we finish his story, is the moment the fire of our fascination with him starts to spark out. That said, we certainly want to shade the character more and more, and we have more hidden facts about him that can slowly come out. We use the word 'he' for shorthand by the way, but The Curious was always meant to transcend such things as pronouns!

-KTH: Despite dealing with fairly dark subject matter, each episode seems to have a moral, or is at least a cautionary tale in some way. Is it important to you that the show maintains that aspect moving forward?

-BB: Interestingly, we never set out to tell moral tales. Not at first. I think you can get a little preachy when you start with morals and come to story second. But what we found was that as we wrote these stories they started to form their own moral, or wrap themselves around one naturally. Turns out there is something very organic about a moral ending - happy or sad, a story can often only end one way, which usually seems to be based on the universal notion of "right" and "wrong." What we don't want to do necessarily, is say what is "fair" and "not fair." We wouldn't like to definitively say Jessie from "Slapstick," or Stu from "Cat Food," or Sam from "Trolled" deserved where they ended up. That's for the audience to decide for themselves.

INTERVIEW WITH ANDY NYMAN

(GHOST STORIES WRITER/PRODUCER/DIRECTOR/STAR)

-Background: In the exceptionally clever anthology, ***Ghost Stories***, the main character listens to several people discuss paranormal encounters in an attempt to disprove them, and in the end discovers some haunting truths about himself. It was very much a collaborative effort between Andy and Jeremy Dyson, and I was humbled to learn about the process of making their very well-reviewed anthology movie.

-Keith Tyler Hopkins: More often than not, the framing narrative in an anthology feels like a means to an end, the end being to get to the next short story. In ***Ghost Stories***, however, the shorts and the framing narrative feel intrinsic to one another. Was this a conscious effort on the part of you and Jeremy?

-Andy Nyman: This element was key to myself and Jeremy. In many portmanteau [anthology] films the flimsy device makes the film simply feel like a series of shorts strung together. Our template was the best of all the anthology films – ***Dead of Night*** (1945). In this remarkable film, the greatest revelation is that the protagonist's story is the best. It also gives meaning to all the other stories and stops them feeling perfunctory.

-KTH: In its tone, ***Ghost Stories*** feels reminiscent of the classic Amicus anthologies. Were you and Jeremy at all influenced by films like ***Asylum*** or ***The House That Dripped Blood***?

-AN: Oh my god, of course! We adore the films of Amicus and Tigon. They are so smart. What they constructed was not only a very entertaining format, but a rather brilliant business model. In shooting essentially short films, it meant you could harness some of the incredible starry actors that happened to be in London as you were only needing them for short bursts. That was something that helped with our casting of the film. The other essential ingredient in those films that was important to us, was the sheer 'Britishness' of them. We didn't want ***Ghost Stories*** to become Americanised, we wanted it to remain true to us and to the spirit of those films we love so much.

-KTH: Part of what I like about your film is that as the audience is brought along on main character Goodman's journey, we question everything we see and everything we're told. Can you articulate why that storytelling style works so well in this film?

-AN: We love the idea of the unreliable witness. What is exciting in the play, and then in the film, is to make Goodman the safe ground which the viewer can rely on. The fun, then, comes in chipping away at that bit by bit so that eventually the audience is in the same situation as Goodman. Staring at a world they thought they understood and realizing that they are hopelessly lost and scared.

-KTH: Having moved ***Ghost Stories*** from the stage to the screen, were there things about working in a different medium that freed the story up to go in new directions? Or, was the switch perhaps constricting in some way?

-AN: Making the change to film was very freeing and a little scary. ***Ghost Stories*** was already an incredibly successful play, so when we came to open it up as a screenplay, it really means starting again. It's very scary to take a format you know 100% works and have to take it apart and throw things out. Once through that fear of course, you end up finding new things that you love.

-KTH: Even though the stage version came out first, was the goal always to make ***Ghost Stories*** as a film?

-AN: No, it was always going to be a play first. The joy of the play was taking the clichés of horror films and putting them on stage. We knew if we could make that work it would be thrilling for an audience to watch.

-KTH: Is there any advice you'd give to a person who wants to adapt their own work to a different medium?

-AN: I guess it's the same advice again and again – Don't write to please anybody but yourself. Write what you would want to go see.

INTERVIEW WITH STEPHEN HAREN

(EDITOR, BLACK MIRROR EPISODE "BLACK MUSEUM")

-Background: I dive deeper into ***Black Mirror*** as a whole in Section II, but the episode that interested me most for this book was "Black Museum." While ***Black Mirror*** is an anthology series in and of itself, "Black Museum" additionally has a self-contained anthology structure. The episode involves a woman, Nish, who is given a tour of a strange museum by a man named Rolo. During the tour, Rolor shares several stories about the museum's artifacts and we transition to short films within the episode. Thus, it's an anthology within an anthology series. Curious about how all of the various storytelling elements were put into practice, I reached out to Stephen Haren, the editor of "Black Museum," to see what he could share about the episode's construction.

-Keith Tyler Hopkins: Can you give some background on how you got the opportunity to edit "Black Museum" for ***Black Mirror***?

-Stephen Haren: I had worked with the Producer previously, and they were looking last minute for an Editor. I was (and am) a great fan of ***Black Mirror*** and so jumped at the chance.

-KTH: When editing for ***Black Mirror***, were you at all focused on the style of previous episodes in the anthology series, or were you allowed to let "Black Museum" be its own thing?

-SH: I was only focused on telling the story in the best possible way. I had seen all previous episodes of ***Black Mirror***, but of course one of the most interesting things about the show is that the episodes are stylistically very different from each other. We were given a great degree of creative freedom and so I was able to help make "Black Museum" feel like its own thing.

-KTH: In an anthology film, it's important that the framing narrative and the short segments drive each other forward, rather than existing in isolation from one another. I think "Black Museum" achieves this quite well. Did you have any conversations with writer Charlie Brooker or director Colm McCarthy about this aspect of the episode?

-SH: I often find anthology-type formats difficult to watch, for the reason that I find my interest levels fluctuating throughout a given film or episode. I may have spoken about this a little with Colm, but it was certainly a great concern of mine privately to make sure that the episode's pace and tone sustained the audience's interest at all times. One of the areas I concentrated on most was integrating the sense of Nish listening to Rolo's storytelling throughout, in the hope that her engagement on screen would in turn encourage engagement for the audience. I also took a lot of care in interweaving Rolo's narration amongst the stories, specifically choosing when to show him onscreen and when to just use his voice. All of this was an attempt to create a very active, driven narrative, despite it necessarily involving a lot of Nish listening onscreen. I was always conscious not to let Nish feel passive, but rather be the audience's eyes and ears to some extent.

Although the structure of the final episode was very similar to the original script, we did remove quite a lot of material in order to not divert too much from the central drive of the story. There were originally some more scenes within Clayton's section, good in their own right, but which for me dragged down the pace and took away from the final switcheroo around Nish. I also felt that by the time you've arrived at a third micro-story, the audience would be in danger of fatigue with the stop/start nature of the structure, and so Clayton's story became a significant area of focus.

-KTH: There's always a risk, when editing an anthology film, to lose the audience's attention in the transition between stories. Do you have any tips for anthology editors about maintaining pace between stories?

-SH: One of the most important things when editing any piece of drama or documentary is to create a sense of flow, a feeling that the story is constantly pushing forward. Anthology films are certainly a challenge in this respect, as they inevitably involve changing gears between stories. The trick is to try and make the gear changes invisible. Looking out for pace and tone changes, pre-lapping dialogue, using stylistic techniques such as slow-motion, speed ramps, jump cuts, dissolves etc. - these tools can all be used to create a fluid and involving narrative. Most important to ask oneself is what is the single, uniting, driving force that you can tap into during the telling of these multiple stories? In a bid to construct one overarching narrative.

INTERVIEW WITH DOUG EMMETT

(ROOM 104 CINEMATOGRAPHER)

-Background: ***Room 104*** is an HBO series that may remind viewers of ***Four Rooms***. Each episode takes place in the same hotel room, but with different characters. The tone of each episode is dictated by the characters it features, so the filmmakers get to dabble in a variety of genres. Of all the movies and series I've analyzed for this book, ***Room 104*** is certainly the least horror-oriented. It ventures into comedy, drama, crime, romance, action, and plenty more genres. That's not to say that there aren't some episodes that flirt with the horror genre. Those watching the first episode of the first season, "Ralphie," might think they're in for a season full of slow-burning scares. In this episode, a babysitter arrives at the hotel room to watch a boy while his father goes out for the night. But the boy has an imaginary friend who shows some dangerous tendencies. Meanwhile, the babysitter has a dark side of her own to contend with. Though ***Room 104*** doesn't have many more horror elements than this, I had a connection with the show's cinematographer and thought he'd be able to share some valuable insights.

Early in our careers, Doug and I had worked together on a small indie drama called ***Fighting Fish*** in upstate New York; me as a grip and he as the cinematographer. On set, he told the story of how he decided to become a cinematographer in film school, and it always stuck with me. When I began working on this book, I hopped onto IMDb to follow up on folks with whom I'd worked in the past, and was amazed to learn that Doug had gone on to shoot ***Paranormal Activity 4***, ***Sorry to Bother You***, and lots of other great films. Having seen ***Room 104***, I knew Doug could offer a ton of insight on what it was like to shoot different stories in different genres on one set, so I sent him an email and a few days later we caught up on the phone.

-Keith Tyler Hopkins: Can you retell me your story about NYU and how you decided to become a cinematographer?

-Doug Emmett: Right. So, freshman year, NYU. The Dean has assembled about three hundred people in an auditorium. We're all freshmen, and she walks out on stage and she goes, how many of you want to be directors? And every hand shot up. Literally, every hand. I look around, and I'm like, oh that dude's got a mohawk and tattoos, and that other guy's got a leather jacket, and that girl's totally cool looking and punk with purple hair. And I'm just like, oh man I don't think I can compete with all these cool people... And then she's like, alright that's great. She goes, how many of you want to be cinematographers? And it's just crickets. And one other hand shoots up.. And I go, sure I'll do this. This is less competition,

-KTH: And how'd you get the opportunity to work on ***Room 104***?

-DE: That came through meeting Mark Duplass. I was shooting a tiny little movie called ***The One I Love***. It was a $100,000 movie. Mark was starring in it and producing it. And he was great. We enjoyed working together. When his cinematographer was not returning for season two of ***Togetherness***, his HBO show, he called me up... He said, would you like to shoot this?

For me that was a huge chance, because I had never shot an HBO TV show. About a year after that the show had been cancelled and he'd always had this idea for this show, ***Room 104***. And HBO said, we'd still love to work with you and we're sorry we're not renewing ***Togetherness***, but if you have anything else let us know. And he's like, I do have something else. Immediately pitched it to them, and they're like, this sounds great.

So, Mark called me back, and immediately I blanched at the idea. Like, I don't know man, I don't know if I can do twelve episodes in a hotel room. I'm thinking Mark is going to want this to look like ***Togetherness***... It was all about the characters and about capturing the dialogue. It was cinematography for utility, which I get, and it serves its purpose. But for me I want to be a little bit more wild and exciting. I said, I can do this show if you'll allow me to make each episode as different and wild looking as possible. And he goes, that's perfect, that's exactly what I want. I was like... great. I'm on board. It was a really fun opportunity to get to work with a bunch of different directors. A lot of them were young indie film directors that were his friends. They gave us three days per episode, which was barely enough time to shoot a half hour of TV. Because we didn't have any location moves we could pull it off. In some cases we even shot two days per episode.

-KTH: I'm really interested in how constraints can sometimes spark creativity... All of a sudden you're on this little soundstage and you're constricted in these ways. Do those constraints lead to happy accidents when it comes to using light and using the camera creatively?

-DE: I think the creative challenge was trying to be different in every episode. The constraint of working in one room was not as challenging as the idea that I had to be as interesting as possible and creatively different across twelve episodes. And so what I did is I mapped it out in advance. And I came up with twelve different, distinct styles of camerawork and lighting. And then I worked with the directors and asked if they were comfortable shooting in that style. It's a little bit of a backwards approach. Usually the director says, hey this is my style and I'd like the cinematographer to accomplish this. But in this scenario we had this kind of strict outline and map that we were gonna take. So each director was totally cool and willing to just sort of say, oh yeah, that style is fine, sure we'll go with it.

-KTH: Oftentimes on a show like this, do you think a director would normally bring on their own DP? Is it kind of unusual to have a consistent DP across all of the episodes that you did?

-DE: In some cases, an anthology, yeah, you would have different DPs come in with their director. I think maybe it was a logistical reason because there were going to be so many different directors that to just streamline the process, maybe having a consistent DP made the most sense.

-KTH: Different film genres, they all have their own visual language, so I wonder if having to dabble in all of these different genres, do you feel like you're a lot more fluent in different film genres now, and you can go out for more diverse gigs?

-DE: The funny thing is the film industry doesn't really work that way. What I think I could do though is if I'm interviewing for a feature film... I don't have a lot of horror stuff on my reel but say I need to interview for a horror film. I'm sure I could use one or two of those episodes that are a little bit darker to use to pitch myself. ***Room 104*** was really great practice to work with a bunch of different directors and to experiment in different styles of cinematography.

But I always feel like the way I get excited about shooting a movie is always based on the script. So I feel like my cinematography, I like for it to be influenced by the script. So I guess it depends. If I got a script that was similar to one of the episodes I might go back to what I had done on ***104*** and think about what worked, what didn't work, and what I'd like to expand upon.

INTERVIEW WITH NICHOLAS PETERSON

(PATIENT SEVEN DIRECTOR)

-Background: Some of the filmmakers interviewed in this book talk about how anthologies cobbled together from premade short films are often not the best. There are, of course, exceptions. I learned from talking with Nicholas Peterson that ***Patient Seven*** was put together in this fashion, but that didn't stop me from enjoying the movie quite a lot.

-Keith Tyler Hopkins: You've done some pretty serious work. You did a little bit of work with Five Finger Death Punch before making the short that wound up in ***Patient Seven***, and then a whole lot of music videos since the short. So how'd you get into the business?

-Nicholas Peterson: I went to CalArts. CalArts is Disney's animation school, unofficially. I did animation there and my first short film went to Sundance and screened in 2000, and from there I started working right out of school in visual effects. I produced visual effects for about 5 or 6 years. Then I raised some money and produced, wrote and directed a feature film called ***Dark Mind*** starring Christopher Masterson and Lyndsy Fonseca. Sold that to a few markets but ultimately realized that independent feature film is really hard to make money with. It takes a really long time and the return is such a slim gamble. I then realized I should probably get into commercials and music videos because the turnaround is much shorter and the budgets are a bit healthier and you can actually make a living making those types of things. So from there I directed a lot of car commercials for Ford and Chrysler, and at the same time, to exercise more creative endeavors, I would do music videos with a much lower budget, but a higher creative outlet. And between that I started doing more short film work to get back into feature films, where I want to work more. And I did that through making a short film with my buddy Jon Heder, who's known as **Napoleon Dynamite**.

I called Jon a couple years ago when Kickstarter had first started. I pitched him a short film called *Drained* and we raised money on Kickstarter and we shot *Drained.* It did really well, I got an agent from it, won a bunch of festivals, and from there we made ***The Visitant***, which is the horror short that's on ***Patient Seven***, with Amy Smart and Doug Jones, again produced with my buddy Jon Heder. And from there I've just been doing more commercials and music videos, and writing and selling and optioning feature film scripts since ***The Visitant*** was produced.

-KTH: When I saw you had Amy Smart and Doug Jones in a short film, I was like, holy crap. Actors that big don't often do shorts. So how were you able to get those guys into the film?

-NP: It was two parts. Jon Heder, he was friends with Doug Jones, 'cause he had done ***Benchwarmers*** and I think something else with Doug. And I'm friends with Steve Wang, and Steve is a creature creator who did ***The Predator***, and ***X-Men,*** and ***Gremlins***, and tons of things... Steve did all the makeup on ***Hellboy***, 'cause Doug is Abe Sapien. So everyone knew everyone. So it came together super fast. And Jon went to his agents and we asked who's available, and they said Amy Smart would love to do this, or potentially do it. So I was on a commercial shoot in New Orleans, and Jon, Amy and I did a phone call, and I pitched Amy the short on the streets of New Orleans while doing this commercial and she said yes and we made the short!

-KTH: It's funny 'cause, of all the Hollywood nightmare stories you hear, it never goes that easy, but a short is a very low time commitment though.

-NP: It is, and that's the thing. A feature film, there's so many variables of agents, lawyers, fees, do they really want to do it, is it going to hurt their career, do I like the director, are they gonna destroy my career? But you're right. A short film, it's very little commitment. It's a day. For this one, two days. And again, Amy liked Jon, she liked Doug, she apparently liked me enough to say yes.

-KTH: So ***The Visitant*** came out two years before ***Patient Seven***. So did you know anything about the anthology, or that there would even be an anthology for this short film when you set out to make it?

-NP: No, I made ***The Visitant*** as a calling card. All short films are calling cards. My agent wanted me to make a calling card, so we made ***The Visitant***. And from there it won festivals, it screened festivals, it was licensed... With short films, you never want to sell them off, unless you're selling the IP [intellectual property] to someone for a lot of money or they're making a feature, which is now happening more. It's kinda rare but that does happen occasionally. Really, you want to own the rights to your short forever and license that out. So, ***Patient Seven*** was just one of the numerous licensing deals I've done with ***The Visitant***. But I did not know about ***Patient Seven*** when I finished it. It came along later.

-KTH: So they distribute it on their end, but then also if you choose to put it on TV or enter it into festivals you can still do that.

-NP: Absolutely, and with each short film deal, certain parameters are windows. For example, El Rey TV, they had an exclusive window for so much time. ***Patient Seven*** had it for so much time, for certain avenues. And you have to navigate those waters because what you don't want to do is do some blanket deal to somebody where they can control it for five or even ten years. Then they're the only ones who can show it. You can't show it anywhere. So you have to be very careful once you are making those deals to do non-exclusive deals and to do deals that make sense for your own exposure.

-KTH: The process of getting into ***Patient Seven***, did they have a competition, or was it you knew someone who knew someone sort of thing?

-NP: They had seen the short at Screamfest and then they approached me afterwards.

-KTH: Is there anything filmmakers should know before contractually getting involved in an anthology?

-NP: The one thing I will say is, and I hadn't seen this before ***Patient Seven***, was you need to make sure that it's clear that they are going to credit you as a filmmaker, as the one who made the shorts within the anthology... but that's another story…

INTERVIEW WITH DAMIEN LEONE

(ALL HALLOWS' EVE & THE TERRIFIER DIRECTOR)

-Background: Art the Clown has become something of an iconic horror character. Though he's best known from 2016's ***The Terrifier***, he actually debuted in short films which were collected in the 2013 anthology, ***All Hallows' Eve***. I was very interested in asking Art's creator about the process of bringing the character from short film to feature film.

-Keith Tyler Hopkins: Did you begin making shorts before you had the idea that they'd end up in an anthology, or was it always your hope that you'd put them together in ***All Hallows' Eve***?

-Damien Leone: As an aspiring filmmaker you typically have no other option but to make short films when you're starting out. I was hoping that a production company would see my short film ***Terrifier*** and offer me funds to turn it into a feature but, for better or worse, things didn't pan out that way. After playing in a few festivals, I eventually uploaded the short to youtube where a producer named Jesse Baget stumbled upon it. He was developing a Halloween horror anthology and scouring the web for pre-made Halloween shorts. ***Terrifier*** was exactly what he was searching for and the project was ***All Hallows' Eve***.

-KTH: Was it always your intent that Art the Clown would spin off into his own feature film, or was that more of a happy accident?

-DL: Art the Clown's first appearance was in my very first short film entitled ***The 9th Circle***. Oddly enough, he was only a supporting character who abducted the protagonist and delivered her into the hands of a Satanic cult. After I showed the film to people, it was pretty unanimous that Art stole the show. He was all everyone kept talking about. After that consensus, the only logical step was to explore his character more in the short film ***Terrifier***. It was my intention with ***Terrifier*** to showcase Art and ultimately raise money for a feature length version.

-KTH: You weren't involved in ***All Hallows' Eve 2*** as a director or a writer. Your sole credit is as a producer. How hands-on were you in that film? At the time that was being made, were you more involved in developing ***The Terrifier*** feature film?

-DL: The producer credit was more of a courtesy to me than anything else since I wrote and directed part 1. My only real contribution to ***All Hallows' Eve 2*** was the construction of the wraparound killer's pumpkin mask. Aside from that, I had no creative input. During that time I was already on my own, developing ***Terrifier*** [the feature].

-KTH: If a filmmaker is making shorts, hoping to someday put them together in an anthology, is there any piece of advice you'd give? Perhaps something you wish you'd done when you first started down this path?

-DL: I wish I wrote better stories and had a lot more money. I was very young when I made my first two short films so I would probably change everything if I could. The only thing I'm truly proud of is the design of Art the Clown. My advice to new filmmakers is just to make films no matter how much money you have. Technically, making films has never been easier than it is today so there's no excuse. All of the equipment is much cheaper and software is much more accessible. Tell a story that really stands out amongst the competition in some way. Luckily, I created a character that resonated with fans of the genre and I provide some decent special effects in my films. Incorporate whatever skills you might have. If you write your own screenplays, focus on that craft more than anything because writing is by far the hardest craft to master. In the end you must eat, breathe and sleep filmmaking. If you're not willing to risk ending up on the street a starving artist, filmmaking is probably not for you.

INTERVIEW WITH P.J. STARKS

(VOLUMES OF BLOOD DIRECTOR)

-Background: P.J.'s first anthology film was shot at a library. (Get it? ***VOLUMES*** *of Blood.*) It surprised me to learn, though, that the library was actually something of a production partner with P.J.

-Keith Tyler Hopkins: So ***Volumes of Blood*** was the product of a class that you held at a public library. Can you break that down for me?

-P.J. Starks: We kind of co-collaborated on this idea called Unscripted Film School and the idea was that we would open it up to do a registration for people in the community who were interested in seeing what it took for an independent film to get made. And they would be able to register and come and work as a production assistant. We also made it a contest where we actually reached out to writers and we did a script writing contest where people could write in…

We got so many requests for production assistants that they actually had to turn people away. So we did that. It was really successful, and then because of that Jim [Davis County Public Library Executive Director] came to me and said… I would like to do the Film School again but let's do something different. I want you to come up with a concept, make it a little bit bigger, a little bit better, and we'll go from there.... So that kind of gave me the opportunity I needed to make that anthology that I had been wanting to make. Plus it was just a really cool opportunity because the library was basically opening its doors and saying, here, do whatever you want to do. And that's basically the genesis of ***Volumes of Blood***...

-KTH: I came from public access television, and I was like, oh man this is like public access TV mentality but towards filmmaking, which is super super cool.

-PJS: What we did differently on the second film school, AKA ***Volumes of Blood***, was because we had so many people reach out and say they wanted to be a part of it the first time we had to turn people away. We didn't have the room for them. What we did differently was we held a registration for every sequence in the movie, and we tried not to bring the same people back over and over and over again to allow new people to come in... I love collaboration and I love working with other people. And that's actually one of the things that I love most about ***Volumes of Blood***. Thanks to the first two films I've worked with probably close to 200 different people in front of the camera and behind the camera. That's just literally what it's about. It's about that collaboration. To me that's what makes it so much fun to work on is that give and take, creating something. Especially with other people who are just as passionate and like-minded.

-KTH: One of the things I'm going to be doing in the book is categorizing anthologies based on their framing devices. But both ***Volumes of Blood*** films, they kind of defy classification. There are films within films, there's campfire-style storytelling, things get meta at times, there's breaking of the 4th wall, there's some nonlinear storytelling. How did you develop such a unique narrative style for these movies?

-PJS: It comes from two places. The first place is, and I'm not trashing other peoples' anthologies, but the one thing for me as a fan of anthology horror films is a lot of the modern anthologies, to me, feel really uninspired. And what I mean by that is it feels like someone says, hey I want to produce a horror anthology and then they get on YouTube and they find five completely random YouTube videos in varied quality that have been done over a period of several years or more... Then they contact those filmmakers and say, hey I'm throwing an anthology together. Do you want to be a part of it? It's like, sure. And you get this random, weird hodge podge, and there's no cohesiveness, there's no interconnectedness, none of that… I've watched anthologies that don't even take the extra step to try to at least come up with some kind of wraparound that makes any kind of sense, or whatever. So I missed those kinds of anthologies, and I wanted to try to do that again.

So that's one place. The other place is, when I came up with the concept for ***Volumes of Blood***... I was like, I'm a horror fan first and foremost. And I have standards and things I love, and I have tropes and things I don't particularly care for... And I wanted, specifically, other fans of the genre, people who love horror films, and love making horror films, to work on the project. And then that way we can all say, here's what we love, here's what we don't love. And then we would try to find a mix of those elements, and those nuances and things like that, and figure out a way that it works best. Not to sound like Bob Ross, but some of the things that happened with ***Volumes of Blood*** came out of happy accidents. Or moments that weren't necessarily anticipated...

-KTH: In the second ***Volumes of Blood***, you kind of took a step back on this one. You didn't direct any segments, right?

-PJS: Right.

-KTH: Was it kind of hard sending you baby off to be taken on by other filmmakers and see it become something maybe you hadn't imagined it would become?

-PJS: At that point not so much… But when you bring others into the fold you have to give up a level of control and you have to start trusting other people. So I had already done that multiple times leading up to the second ***Volumes of Blood***. And I had done that quite a bit on the first one because I had written a majority of the stories and come up with the concept and all that stuff. So I had already handed a lot of that over to the other directors on the first film. When it was all said and done, I thought they all did a fantastic job with what they were given and in some cases they came up with ideas that weren't there originally, or they added on certain characterizations, or they added more to a character, and that kind of thing. I'm completely 100% open to ideas from anybody. If the guy just cleaning up pools of blood is like, you know what, I've got an idea, I listen to that. Because at the end of the day, as creative as I might be, everybody else working on the project is equally a creative entity. So it would be dumb to not listen to other people's ideas…

-KTH: What advice would you give to a filmmaker who's wanting to craft the frame story for their own anthology?

-PJS: When it comes to creating the framework for what is an anthology, it's like, how can you take something that's been done a gazillion times already and put your own spin on it to where you're not just redoing ***Tales from the Darkside*** or ***After Midnight***... So many films have been done. It can be tough to come up with something that's wholly original... Don't necessarily do it from a place, I gotta be better than this guy. I have to be 100% fresh, because by incorporating things in there that other horror fans love, they'll be able to connect with those moments. And if you can put your own spin on it. If you can take a trope that's been done a hundred times and then… incorporate your own voice into it, I really think that's the best route to go. And if you can somehow manage to create a cohesiveness, a wraparound story that not only works on its own as a separate story, but at the same time can combine elements from the other stories to where in some way it's interwoven, or somehow connected, I think that's the best route to go.

INTERVIEW WITH SOFIA CARRILLO

(XX WRAPAROUND DIRECTOR)

-Background: *XX* is billed as the first horror anthology made entirely by female directors, but that's only one reason to check out this multi-layered anthology. Sofia Carrillo directed several stop motion animation segments that bookend each short film. These segments are abstract, dreamlike, and creepy as hell. Sofia's segments are so elusive in their meaning that I had to reach out to her and see how she put them together.

-Keith Tyler Hopkins: How did you come to be involved in directing the wraparound segments for ***XX***?

-Sofia Carrillo: I met Todd Brown [*XX* Producer] I think in 2010 and he saw my work and I think he really liked it. We kept in touch. When I was releasing new short films I used to send them to him, so were we really in touch, we were close. After six years he asked me to work with this project and it was kind of a very nice experience, but also, it was surprising for me. I mean, he used to say names like Karyn Kusama [*XX* Segment Director] and in those times there were also the Soska sisters [***American Mary***, ***The ABCs of Death 2***]. For me it was kind of a fantasy you know? It was like, I'm not sure if this is true but I'm going to keep working. And I think we wrote, like, two years.

And after two years the project was ready to go on. And in fact, I said no. Because it was two years, so at some point I just decided I couldn't go on because I was facing another short film. So I was in two different productions so it was very hard for me. And I said no, but after, perhaps it was two weeks, I realized that some of my crew had to go work on other things. So I just decided to go again and ask Todd if I could go again with the project and he said yes. So that's a little bit of how it happened.

-KTH: So did they really tell you what should be in your segments or did you have freedom to do whatever you wanted to?

-SC: He told me about the dollhouse and he also told me about how each room was one segment. It was a very good idea, but I said okay no, I'm going to go with my own idea <laughs>. And I pitched them the idea. They said yes. And a few months later I just decided to go again with the first idea but mixed with my idea. So at the end it is a kind of a mixture of the first idea and my idea... I was really excited about making this mixture and in the end I really like it and I think they also like it... I had so much freedom, and they really respect my work. So it was a great experience because, I said, okay now I'm going to try this. And I used to send them pictures of the process of making the puppets and he said, okay! You know, like, every time! Because I wanted to do a great job and so I was kind of insecure sometimes. But they were so respectful with my freedom and with my aesthetic. It was a great experience.

-KTH: The idea of a dollhouse inside a house reminds me of an anthology, because an anthology is a film within a film. Was any of that intentional of your part?

-SC: No, it was not intentional because I had so little information about the segments. I had mostly a one sentence description of the short idea. I didn't have any image or mood board from those short films, so I was really blind and just trusting.

-KTH: That's very cool because in the end everything feels very cohesive. When I was watching the film, and I've watched the film several times, I kind of figured that you maybe had at least scripts or something. Because the whole thing does have a togetherness about it.

-SC: Well it's great to hear that because I only had, like one sentence. He told me, like, Karyn Kusama's is about a ***Rosemary's Baby*** kid growing up. And Jovanka Vuckovic's is about a box. It was just one sentence. And also, Roxanne Benjamin's segment, Roxanne and Annie Clark were the last two segments... So, when they came into the project I already had their vignettes. So in the case of Roxanne it is kind of magic that it really fit... Because I didn't have the sentence. So I made them blind. Absolutely blind.

-KTH: What was it like to have directed a part of the first horror anthology film that was directed by all women?

-SC: Well I think, as I told you at the beginning, for me, being a Mexican animator doing experimental things I was not really aware of the importance of this anthology until we presented it in Sundance. When we premiered the movie in Sundance I really realized that this was the first anthology made only by women and I was really thankful in life to have this opportunity. Because in animation sometimes it's like, we live in an alone world. And the fiction, live action world, it is very different. So when we finished the anthology I had this sense of the difficulties of working in live action as being a woman and trying to work in horror movies. I realized that this was a real great idea. So for me, I think, when we premiered in Sundance it was all around this protest against Trump.

-KTH: The March for Women?

-SC: Exactly. So that day, that precise day, we premiered the movie and oh my God, I was like, this is huge. This is, like, historical. And I think I feel grateful and very happy to be involved in this anthology. I'm really proud. And also, that day I realized that I was a woman animator making these vignettes for the first anthology of horror made only by women. Also I was a Mexican animator. There was this big thing with Trump against Mexicans and I was there working in this production and also premiering that day. So for me I have to say that it was one of the strong things that I have done in 2017.

-KTH: As someone who works mostly in short form, why do you like short films and do you think that you'll ever direct a feature film entirely by yourself?

-SC: I've been working in short form because I'm in love with short stories. I've written short stories. That was my first love. I wanted to be a writer and I wanted to make short stories. I think it's also because making stop motion animation is really hard and it is faster to work in a short film... This year I'm working on two scripts for feature animated films. So yes, it's my next stop. And I think I get energy from the anthology to make my work and I've kind of fallen in love with cinema. I've always been in love with cinema but I think to have been involved in a feature, I really want to do this in a professional way and I want to do this my whole life. So that was also important about working in that film.

This year I made my first live action short film and it's also about fantasy and it's also about kind of a horror thing. That also happened because I was in touch with Jovanka Vuckovic [***XX*** director] and the other directors also. I really got close to Jovanka and kind of inspired. And I want to do movies! I want to do features! Of course I'm going to keep going with short films because those are tiny and you can be experimental... There's a lot of freedom in the short form that you can't use in long-form.

-KTH: For a filmmaker who is just starting out, would you encourage them, or why would you encourage them to get involved in an anthology film?

-SC: When you do a feature you have to work with other people, so there's this collaborative process with very talented people. And this is not work like if you were a painter. Right? All alone in your studio. So working in an anthology, it's very rich because it is, like I said, if you make a movie with these talented people, but there's these tiny cells working in just one project. I think that it is a great experience but also you have to be very aware of what kind of anthology you are working. For me it was a surprising gift because it was about women and because there was this idea in the whole project to work for women. We wanted to help each other and we wanted to push each other. So if you are going to work in an anthology, I suggest not *only* to do it because it's a faster way to a feature film. You should be very comfortable with what it is about.

INTERVIEW WITH MICHAEL MCQUOWN

(THE DARK TAPES DIRECTOR)

-Background: Michael McQuown's indie anthology is much more than your average found footage horror film. It explores dreams in multiple timelines and in multiple planes of reality. To me it actually felt more like a Christopher Nolan movie than a typical horror film. It was fun to talk with him about how he used found footage tropes to make such a complex movie.

-Keith Tyler Hopkins: What first made you interested in directing a horror anthology film?

-Michael McQuown: I had friends telling me I should direct something. I had shot something on video in the 90s so I was familiar with the process. But I told them, look, doing a full feature is tough. It would be like trying to run a marathon without training. So, I didn't want to do a short because there would really be no way to monetize a short. But I thought, okay, if we do an anthology, that way it's a series of shorts. And if we mess up one of the shorts -kinda like if you mess up the beginning of your training- then we can go back and reshoot it. So that was on the top of my head, and then when I saw ***V/H/S***, and I've said this in other interviews, I immediately turned to two friends and I said, oh, we're gonna do an anthology like ***V/H/S***. I said we could do it as a crew of just two or three of us if we do found footage. So that's why it was found footage, influenced from ***V/H/S***. But we tried to do stories that were different, that people hadn't seen. One of the problems, I think, with anthologies is that they often are just a scene, whereas I try to do mini features if that makes any sense.

-KTH: Where did you start in production? Did you start with the shorts, or did you come up with the idea for the wraparound and then make the shorts?

-MM: We shot "Hunters and Hunted" first. That was the first story you see in its entirety, front to end. And then I knew I wanted to do one that involved cams, so I thought of the concept of "Cam Girls" shortly thereafter. And I then thought of the concept of "Amanda's Revenge." And "To Catch a Demon," which ended up being the wraparound. I had a one-time experience of night terrors where I saw a black figure. This happened to me right after college. So what the professor is saying is often the words I told to people trying to explain it. And the whole scientific theory that the professor explains is just something that I thought up of to explain the terrors. In terms of the wraparound, we actually shot part of a separate wraparound as I was editing.

The Dark Tapes was shot over a period of two years, so as I was editing everything I thought, "To Catch a Demon" would work better as a wraparound and we broke it up into chunks rather than back to back like the other stories. And after that I actually thought, we can tie it into the stories this way. So it was after we shot everything that I thought to make "To Catch a Demon" the wraparound. And then the demon's voice that you hear at the beginning and the end of the film… What the demon was saying, I further tried to make an anthology that would connect to the wraparound and a wraparound that would connect to the stories.

-KTH: I was actually going to ask you about "The Hunters and the Hunted," because that's the only one that kind of breaks the mold in terms of, it ends up being human perpetrators rather than some sort of demonic perpetrator. That all makes sense when I learn that that was the first one you made.

-MM: Yeah that was the first one we made and then again, we didn't have the concept of the wraparound. And then if you do watch the credits, I don't know if you ended up watching the credits, the demon voice comes back on and says, "we influence many into evil." I think that's the exact line. And then you see flashes of some of the people in "The Hunters and the Hunted," so that's how I was sort of tying it in. So that was the first one we shot and that also ended up being one of the ones that people liked the most, so rather than messing up the first one, having to reshoot it, we ended up doing a really good one for the first one.

-KTH: "To Catch a Demon" was the only segment in which you brought on a second director. As the primary director of the film, what's your approach to that? Were you very hands on, or were you kinda hands off, and just said, bring back what you bring back?

-MM: So we met. I got a referral over to Vincent [J. Guastini], and we had already shot "Hunters and Hunted." I didn't want the movie to be a lot of gore, but I wanted whatever bloody or gory effects we had to be done to be done well. So we got a referral to Vincent and he liked everything. He said he would come on board for a very good rate if he could shoot one of the segments. So I told him about the segments that we had planned and he really liked "To Catch a Demon." So my friends that were helping me ended up crewing with Vincent, and he also brought in his own director of photography and stunt person, and then my friends were helping him. And then, yeah, I was just sort of producing so I was just on the side coordinating everything.

-KTH: ***The Dark Tapes*** plays with time in a way that fascinated me, especially in the final moments. It's got this kind of ***Memento*** or ***Inception*** kind of ending. And that's kind of unusual in horror anthologies. What was your approach to doing a nonlinear film?

-MM: Well you can see that I'm a fan of science fiction. I'm a fan of Hitchcock and murder mysteries. So by not being just a horror fan, I guess you could say that's how the influence came in. So when I list the film I'll often say it's a horror, sci-fi, thriller or mystery film because it's got elements of all of those in there.

-KTH: Another thing that I think makes ***The Dark Tapes*** interesting is that there's a wraparound with the two people discovering the trashed theater, but then "To Catch a Demon," it's also a wraparound in and of itself.

-MM: I kind of say that "To Catch a Demon" is the wraparound. And the people discovering the theater, which actually was going to be the wraparound. We shot some other stuff there, and then when I thought of "To Catch a Demon" I thought it was an improvement on it. So we just ditched the stuff we had shot with them and kept them discovering the camera. But I say it's more like bookends holding everything together.

-KTH: What I really like about it is, sometimes you see a nonlinear film and the scenes are just jumbled, but in this case the nonlinear approach suits the subject matter and suits the storytelling.

-MM: I've always been a fan of ***The Twilight Zone***, and when I was a kid in the 80s there was a bunch of anthology films that came out and I always enjoyed those. So you can see a little bit of the influences there. But I certainly would say, if you're an up and coming filmmaker, and it doesn't have to be horror necessarily, an anthology is certainly one way to do something. Like I said, if you mess up one of the stories you can always go back and reshoot it, whereas you don't have that capability to do it on an entire feature.

-The takeaway: Michael bringing on a guest director reminds me of ***Sin City***, in which Robert Rodriguez brought on Quinten Tarantino to direct a scene. The willingness to share a segment of your anthology with another director shows a great deal of humility. My anthology, ***Gravedigger Dave's Halfway House***, probably would have benefited from that level of maturity. Nevertheless, I'm glad I decided to go down that road for the sequel, ***Gravedigger Dave Meets His Match***.

INTERVIEW WITH AL JEAN

(THE SIMPSONS "TREEHOUSE OF HORROR" WRITER/PRODUCER)

-Background: For me, ***The Simpsons***' annual Halloween specials were my earliest exposure to the horror tropes I now adore. When I was a kid I actually found the "**Treehouse of Horror**" episodes really scary. And I enjoyed their structure, which included several short stories in one episode. Even then, their similarity to an evening of stories around a campfire wasn't lost on me.

Al Jean has worked on ***The Simpsons*** as writer, producer, and/or showrunner since 1989. Reaching out to someone of his stature was a real shot in the dark (so I had editor Matthew Dressel do it for me). I was thrilled and somewhat starstruck when he said he'd answer some questions. He was concise in his responses, but I'm incredibly grateful that he responded at all.

-Keith Tyler Hopkins: You've been involved in the "**Treehouse of Horror**" episodes since the beginning. Can you tell me about the first special got off the ground?

-Al Jean: I've been involved in every "**Treehouse**" except 7 and 8 (which were excellent). The first special was worrisome; it was definitely scarier than any cartoon that had aired on a network before then. Jim Brooks

[Writer/Producer] thought Marge should give a warning, which she did for a couple seasons until we figured everyone knew what they were in for. Recently we had Lisa give a warning before the segment where Homer ate himself. But TV as a whole is a lot grosser now. The first episode Matt [Groening, ***Simpsons*** Creator] also had some concerns that "The Raven" played it a little too straight so we had a quick rewrite with Jim and Matt where Mike Reiss pitched the Raven saying "eat my shorts."

-KTH: These specials initially featured framing narratives that would tie the breakout segments together, making them one story. At a certain point the episodes stopped including a framing narrative. Can you talk about why the change was made?

-AJ: We initially had a framing narrative but as the shows got shorter it seemed like we could get more bang for our buck by having a funny cold open. Originally the segments had three separate writers and three separate directors. When we joined the writers guild that became much more expensive so we had one credited writer although everyone pitches in.

-KTH: As "**Treehouse of Horror**" episodes are very rooted in the horror genre, and most ***Simpsons*** episodes are not, does the writer's room have a different vibe during the process of making these specials?

-AJ: There's a lot of excitement among the writers and directors for the "**Treehouse**" episodes; some because of the horror genre but more because of the freedom of three unrelated acts which obey fewer rules and in many cases are based on a classic story. The "**Treehouse**" episodes are written a year in advance in order to give the character designers and directors as much time as possible. With regard to "current" movies it's hard to know what "current" really means for a show that airs in syndication. Some said when we did an ***E.T.*** parody it was "dated" but no one had that concern when we parodied ***The Shining*** 14 years after the film. We never hold back on obscure references and we feel that just as ***Mad Magazine*** introduced us to adult movies as a kid the "**Treehouse**" specials might serve as a child's introduction to Cthulu.

-The Takeaway: Perhaps there isn't much above in the way of actionable advice for indie filmmakers, but if you think you have nothing to learn from the "**Treehouse**" specials you're certainly mistaken. The way in which elements of parody, trope, homage, and actual scares are weaved into these episodes reflect anthology storytelling at it's finest. And they're also hilarious.

As "**Treehouse of Horror**" was my introduction to the horror anthology format, this seems like a good point to move on to Section II, where we'll look at the story structure of a plethora of anthology films and series.

SECTION II: THE FILMS

(REFERENCE & ACTIONABLE TAKEAWAYS FOR FILMMAKERS)

This reference section is not exhaustive by any means. The number of independent horror anthologies available has skyrocketed in recent years, and it would've been impossible to include all of them. My attempt here is to include the ones that will be most important to the form in the years ahead. These films and series are listed chronologically, but categorized based on the style of their wraparound. These wraparound styles are defined below:

STORYTELLING

This describes anthologies in which the audience watches a dramatization of a story being told by one character to another. It also includes anthologies in which shorts are dramatized from stories that characters read out of books, either silently or aloud. A good example in film would be ***Tales from the Hood***, in which a mortician tells stories about his recent "customers" to a group of thugs. A good example from TV is ***Are You Afraid of the Dark?***, in which a group of kids gather around a fire every week to tell each other scary stories.

The distinguishing feature that separates Storytelling anthologies from Horror Host anthologies is that characters in Storytelling anthologies do not break the "fourth wall." The fourth wall, in filmmaking, describes the point of view of the camera, and the fourth wall is said to be broken when a character looks into the lens and directly addresses the audience. Good examples of Hosted anthology series are ***The Twilight Zone*** and ***Tales from the Crypt***. So, the primary difference between Storytelling and Hosted anthologies comes from the perspective of the audience. In Storytelling anthologies, the person being told the story is a character in the film. In Horror Host anthologies, the person being told the story is you, the viewer.

Storytelling is the oldest wraparound style in the horror anthology subgenre, going back to ***Unheimliche Geschichten*** (1919), ***Waxworks*** (1924), and ***Dead of Night*** (1945). Despite their age, these early horror films still inform modern filmmakers. The acclaimed 2017 anthology, ***Ghost Stories***, was particularly influenced by ***Dead of Night.*** As writer/director/star Andy Nyman told me, “In this remarkable film, the greatest revelation is that the protagonist’s story is the best. It also gives meaning to all the other stories and stops them feeling perfunctory.”

It’s a similar logic that led me to using this wraparound style in ***Gravedigger Dave’s Halfway House***. For my money, Storytelling anthologies are particularly likely to have meaningful wraparounds, as opposed to wraparounds that simply navigate from short to short. Some of my favorite Storytelling anthologies include ***Asylum*** and ***Tales from the Darkside: The Movie*** precisely because they feature the same revelation that Nyman saw in

Dead of Night. They each feature a protagonist that has something to gain from telling, or listening to, the stories.

MIND'S EYE

This wraparound style includes anthologies in which something a character remembers or imagines is depicted in a short film. While such wraparound segments feel similar to Storytelling segments, the difference is that nothing is spoken aloud or read by the wraparound characters. Instead, the short film exists only within a character's mind, and the other characters are not privy to it.

Though I've categorized Mind's Eye as a distinct wraparound style, you'll often see it in anthologies that also utilize a Storytelling style. This occurs in one of the earliest anthology films, ***Waxworks***. In this silent film, the first few shorts are read by a woman in the wraparound, but the last occurs in a dream.

HORROR HOSTS

In the first episode of ***Alfred Hitchcock Presents***, Hitchcock tells the audience that he won't be acting in these episodes, but instead will be serving as, "something of an accessory before and after the fact." This sums up the role of the horror host quite nicely. They exist to give the audience context, as well as a sense of connective tissue between otherwise unconnected narratives. From here, Hitchcock gets humorously condescending, explaining that he's here, "to give the title to those of you who can't read, and tidy up afterwards for those who don't understand."

Though this seems a bit patronizing, what he's really getting at is that the most essential function of such a host is to provide levity. TV horror hosts are best known for providing segue skits between commercial breaks during b-movies and cheesy horror flicks. As stated by several modern TV horror hosts in the wonderful 2006 documentary, ***American Scary***, this TV trope is simply a modern manifestation of the "literary guide." This type of character has existed in storytelling as far back as history can record, and television's original horror hosts, like **Vampira** and **Roland** (AKA **Zacherley**), took their characters very seriously. They seldom ventured into farce and played them as realistically as possible. It's not that there weren't jokes. There were always jokes, but they were played without the self-conscious wink that's now common to the trope.

Almost simultaneously, another brand of TV horror host was forming; one most commonly associated with Rod Serling in ***The Twilight Zone.*** His serious tone was also prevalent in other anthology shows of the era, like ***13 Demon Street*** and ***One Step Beyond***, as well as later shows, like ***Unsolved Mysteries***.

For the horror hosts that would follow, like **Elvira** and **Svengoolie**, campiness became increasingly inherent to the form. In our Section I interview, **Crematia Mortem** herself likened it to, "whistling in the graveyard."

EC Comics titles of the 1950s, like ***Tales from the Crypt*** and ***Vault of Horror***, featured horror hosts, and continue to be influential on anthology filmmakers. Both of these titles would be adapted to film, and their general style has been hugely influential on the ***Creepshow*** franchise. These EC horror comics featured hosts that helped readers navigate between the several stories that would appear in each issue. In the documentary, ***Tales from the Crypt: From Comic Books to Television***, comic historian Jerry Weist says, "By using the horror host, EC kept a perspective on what they were doing and they reminded their readers that this was fiction, and it was entertainment." I couldn't have said it better.

FILM WITHIN A FILM

Anthologies all feature films within films, don't they? So why should I even bother identifying this as a wraparound category? It's because in these anthologies, the shorts are being watched by characters in the wraparound, and these characters are fully aware that they're watching something produced by a film crew. An early example is 1983's ***Screamtime***.

In this film, a pair of hoodlums steal a bunch of VHS tapes from a video store and bring them to a gal's apartment. Like the ***All Hallows' Eve*** films, which would follow many years later, the short films take on a supernatural quality, coming to life and reaching out of the TV to attack the characters from the frame story.

A more recent use of this wraparound style can be found in 2019's ***Nightmare Cinema***. This anthology centers around an ornate cinema that has an uncanny ability to lure certain people into screenings. Each time a person enters, a short film begins that shows their fate.

Film Within a Film anthologies shouldn't be confused with Found Footage anthologies, in which the shorts have a raw, unedited feel. Anthologies falling in the Film Within a Film category include shorts that are more polished. The characters in these wraparounds know they're watching short films, not raw footage that was never meant to be found.

One 80s anthology series that utilizes the premise that the audience is watching each short with the characters is ***Monsters***. In the open, we descend on a seemingly normal suburban neighborhood and enter an ordinary suburban home. Inside, we see three monsters behaving as we might expect a family of humans to behave. As they gather around the TV they remark that their favorite show is on, "Monsters." As they sit back and watch evil humans doing evil things, we see the TV from their perspective.

FOUND FOOTAGE

The Found Footage anthologies analyzed in this book, most notably ***V/H/S***, utilize a similar technique as the aforementioned ***Monsters***. In ***V/H/S***, the wraparound characters find stacks of VHS tapes with raw, seemingly unedited footage. Though *we* see them as short films helmed by a director, the characters in the anthology view the tapes as footage that was most definitely not meant to be viewed by an audience. This is a key differentiation between Found Footage anthologies and Film Within a Film anthologies, but not the only one. The aesthetic is also important.

Found Footage anthologies are allowed to look like crap. In fact, they're supposed to look like crap. This highlights the wonderful thing about (and perhaps the problem with) found footage filmmaking. The barrier to entry is very low. Independent filmmakers can use whatever camera is at the ready to make a found footage movie, but I'd always wondered how a studio movie might approach it.

When I had cinematographer Doug Emmett on the phone to talk about ***Room 104***, the conversation veered to ***Paranormal Activity 4***, which he also shot. I was curious about whether the budget of $5 million (big when compared to many of the films analyzed here) would allow the crew to shoot on nicer equipment. I said to Doug, "I wondered if you'd shot it on an Alexa or something and then crapped it up in post."

He replied, "The best thing to do if you want a specific look for your movie, just shoot with that camera… So we used Panasonic HD, I think at the time they were probably 1080 cameras."

As far as sound is concerned, Doug told me, "the editor wanted to use the onboard sound from the microphone of the camera even though we had a boom operator for the whole thing."

The gear needed to make a movie distributed by Paramount Pictures can be found in any pawn shop. That's why it's so important that Found Footage anthologies be clever and unique.

PACKAGE FILMS

When I use the term, Package Film anthology, I'm describing a collection of shorts bundled into a feature-length release. With the absence of any sort of filmed framing device, these anthologies play almost like a screening session at a film festival. Rather than any sort of framing, simple uses of titles and credits indicate to the viewer that one short has ended and another will begin.

The true nature of the Package Film anthology is perhaps best illustrated by the DVD menu of the 1968 anthology, ***Spirits of the Dead***. While initially released theatrically as one complete film, the DVD menu first lists each short individually. The final option allows the viewer to, "play all." A Package Film anthology watched from beginning to end is akin to hitting the "play all" button on a DVD, or a mixtape, or a playlist.

On the studio level, Package Film anthologies are sometimes released to expand upon a popular intellectual property. Some mainstream examples include ***The Animatrix*** and ***Batman: Gotham Knight***, both of which were direct-to-DVD releases that served to fill the gap between theatrically released franchise films. In the indie world, the way in which the shorts are collected varies a great deal, from directors looking to showcase their work, to producers taking open submissions (as they might with a film festival).

For a Package Film anthology that was released as a compilation of a filmmaker's early work, refer to Alex Ferarri's ***Lipstick and Bullets***. If you haven't listened to Ferrari's amazing podcast, ***Indie Film Hustle***, you probably should. Aside from conducting incredibly insightful interviews with a wide range of professionals in the industry, Ferrari often discusses his own filmmaking experiences, including the compilation of four of his shorts.

Originally released separately, the shorts were repackaged on DVD and billed as "a collection of revenge films." And watching these shorts it's easy to detect a thematic throughline, particularly in his "Red Princess" shorts. Curious about how this anthology came to be, I reached out to Ferrari, and was not shocked to learn that it wasn't his original intent to make an anthology.

He told me over email about a narrative feature he'd planned to make with the characters in his shorts:

> Something about revenge always fascinated me so I explored it… I had an entire world locked and loaded for Red Princess Blues but I could never find the financing I needed to move forward… I really never had any

> plans to create an anthology but since the theme and tone was there I ran with it.

In retrospect though, Ferrari does have some advice to filmmakers making shorts with the intent of grouping them later:

> Try to create films that are the same tone and style. If you can have a uniting element (think ***Four Rooms***) all the better. I wish I would've focused on a more connected storyline between all the films.

But perhaps a connected storyline isn't what you're after. As writer/producer Charlie Brooker said in an interview with Digital Spy, "***Black Mirror*** is a flavor." While package films don't necessarily have to have any narrative throughline, I think a consistent flavor is a good idea.

If you have that going for you, it may be that a simple chronological ordering of your shorts is a great way to showcase your development (and release a feature). And if you'd prefer your short films to be viewed as individual works rather than small parts of a larger whole, this wraparound-style could serve as your template.

THEMATIC THROUGHLINE

This describes films and series in which the shorts are linked by similarities in subject matter, mood, locations, characters, or other elements. Anthologies in this wraparound category often don't have a linkage that's as on-the-nose as the others.

Oftentimes, due to the nature of thematically linked anthologies, they don't actually require the use of a frame story. Some examples include, ***The ABCs of Death*** franchise and ***Holidays***, which don't feature a traditional wraparound. They rather feature graphical intros and outros for each short. While these may seem fairly similar to Package Film anthologies, the common thread between the shorts is what differentiates Thematic Throughline anthologies.

In ***Holidays***, for instance, each short takes place on a different holiday. In ***The ABCs of Death***, the title of each short begins with a different letter, and shorts are ordered alphabetically. While Package Film anthologies may certainly have a theme, it's not as prevalent as in Thematic Throughline anthologies.

TANGENTIAL THROUGHLINE

The wraparound categories described thus far have been rather simple, at least in terms of plot. Most are fairly straightforward, and feature a return to a familiar wraparound in between each short or episode to help the viewer feel grounded. In Tangential Throughline anthologies, however, the filmmakers allow the viewer to come untethered from any familiar ground.

These films usually don't have a wraparound, or at least not one that remains consistent for the duration of the film. Structurally, they are free to go anywhere. The Tangential Throughline anthology structure lends itself to genres outside of horror. You'll find no better and example than the 1995 comedy anthology film, ***Four Rooms***. The shorts in this film are tied together by a hotel bellhop who encounters a number of bizarre guests over a single shift. With four directors at the helm, including genre masters Robert Rodriguez and Quinten Tarantino, ***Four Rooms*** is a shining example of a tangential anthology that, against all odds, feels cohesive.

Rodriguez's comic book neo-noirs ***Sin City*** and ***Sin City: A Dame to Kill For*** are also perfect examples of plot structures that I define as being tangential. Both movies spins yarns that intersect this way and that, without ever tying all storylines into a singular knot. The same can be said of Richard Linklater's acclaimed indies ***Slacker*** and ***Waking Life***, in which the narrative floats from conversation to conversation with a sort of reckless abandon, not concerned with building a cohesive plot, but rather a cohesive philosophy. The Cohen brothers' 2018 western, ***The Ballad of Buster Scruggs***, likewise meanders between unconnected stories and characters, all the while building on the notion that the stories are part of a shared universe.

Though similar in a variety of ways, tangential anthologies should not be confused with films like ***Crash***, ***Traffic***, and ***Magnolia***, which have been labeled as "Hyperlink Cinema." Coined by Alissa Quart, the term describes a method of interlocking various narratives that seem disparate at first, but converge as the film progresses. While all of the aforementioned films are magnificent in their own way, my interest here is horror, and we have several Tangential Throughline anthologies to look at.

The wraparound categories outlined above aren't absolutes. The lines between one or the other are often blurry, as many anthologies use a variety of wraparound techniques. Nevertheless, with the aforementioned wraparound styles in mind, peruse the anthology films deconstructed in the rest of this section. Pay special attention to plot and story structure, always keeping in mind how you might be able to put your own spin on the horror anthology subgenre.

THE SILENT ERA - 1960s

UNHEIMLICHE GESCHICHTEN (FILM, 1919)

1 DIRECTOR | RUNTIME: 1HR 38MIN

-Notable Cast/Crew: Actors Anita Barber, Reinhold Schünzel, & Conrad Veidt

-Wraparound type: Storytelling, Mind's Eye

-The Setup: This film's German title roughly translates to "Eerie Stories," or "Spooky Stories." It takes place in a book shop, as three portraits come to life after the store has closed and the patrons have vacated. Human forms step out of each of the portraits and they all spend the night reading short tales of death, crime, and mischief. As they read, the audience sees each tale through the character's mind's eye. Supporting this concept, the three actors who play the waking portraits, Anita Barber, Reinhold Schünzel, and Conrad Veidt, also star in the shorts. Hence, the characters of the frame story are imagining themselves as the characters about which they read.

-First short: A husband and wife are enjoying a stay at a hotel. When the wife disappears, the husband is baffled that the hotel staffers deny her very existence.

-Second short: Two men competing for the same woman roll dice over her. Enraged, the loser strangles the winner to death, but is then haunted by his enemy's ghost.

-Third short: In this adaptation of Edgar Allan Poe's "The Black Cat," an abusive alcoholic murders his wife and hides her body in the basement walls.

-Fourth short: A detective who uncovers a suicide cult is chosen to be their next sacrifice, and must outsmart the cult's leader to stay alive.

-Fifth short: A man competing with his rival for a woman's affection stages paranormal pranks in an attempt to scare him off.

-Return to wraparound: In between each short, the characters revel in the evils about which they read, until, at the end of the film, the shop owner arrives with the authorities. Although the shop is trashed, the three culprits have gone missing. As soon as the police leave, it all clicks for the store owner. He approaches each of the three portraits and eyes them suspiciously. To his horror, the figures in the portraits all take a moment to jeer at him until he comically runs off in terror and the anthology comes to an end.

-The Takeaway: In this movie, the first horror anthology film according to my research, we're given a structural template that is still used today. This film introduces a group of characters that are bound to a single setting, and tells stories from their perspectives. It's so simple, but one film had to do it first. Be sure to give this one a watch, even if only for historical context. We might not even have a horror anthology subgenre if not for this groundbreaking silent film.

• • •

WAXWORKS (FILM, 1924)

1 DIRECTOR | RUNTIME: 1HR 14MIN

-Notable Cast/Crew: Actor Conrad Veidt

-Wraparound type: Storytelling, Mind's Eye

-The Setup: In this German silent film, a writer responds to a wax museum's help-wanted ad. The museum is looking for writers to create background stories for their sculptures. The museum's proprietor takes the writer on an introductory tour of his work, at which point the audience is introduced to the figures that'll be the main characters of the shorts: Springheeled Jack, Ivan the Terrible, and Harun-Al Raschid- Caliph.

Interestingly, the order in which they're introduced does not dictate the order of the shorts, for just as the introductions have concluded, an arm falls off Harun's sculpture, prompting the writer to get started on that story first.

As the writer crafts the story, the proprietor's daughter watches excitedly over his shoulder. It's from her perspective, as she reads the words he's putting to paper, that we transition to the first short. Through this technique, the audience watches the story through her mind's eye as she imagines his words brought to life.

-First short: Harun had a different wife for every day of the year, but coveted the local baker's wife most of all. On the same night that Harun sneaks out of the palace to pursue the baker's wife, the baker sneaks into the palace to murder Harun. Calamity ensues when neither plot goes as planned.

-Return to wraparound: After this first short, we go back to the frame story to re-establish that the woman is still reading the writer's words.

-Second short: Ivan the Terrible revels in torture. With a poison maker as his alchemist, and The Devil and Death as his chief aids, Ivan decrees that whomever's name is written on the alchemist's hourglass shall be the next to die when the sand runs out. Fearing for his own life at Ivan's hands, the alchemist write's Ivan's name on the hourglass, hoping to drive the man into a state of panic.

-Return to wraparound: The writer is satisfied with his work and stacks the sheets of his finished stories. But when he looks for the woman, he sees that she's gone to sleep. At this point the anthology takes an unexpected turn. Exhausted, the writer falls asleep. Instead of writing his third story, about Springheeled Jack, he instead dreams of it, allowing us to see this last one from his perspective rather than the woman's.

-Third short: In this much shorter short, Jack's ghost chases the writer and the woman through a carnival.

-Return to wraparound: The writer wakes up abruptly, and is relieved to learn that it had all been a dream. In true silent-era fashion, the writer and the woman kiss as the film comes to a close.

-The takeaway: It's funny how much shorter this third segment is, and how different it is from the previous two. It's a very sudden change in format, and it's never clear whether the writer's dream will have any bearing on the story he'll eventually write for Springheeled Jack. It does something interesting to the pacing of this anthology, ramping up the intensity just before the movie ends. Including this short at the beginning of this film would have been a mistake. It would've set the pace too fast. Finishing with it, however, ends the anthology on a high note.

I was actually somewhat relieved to find a classic anthology film with a short under five minutes. Prior to completing ***Gravedigger Dave's Halfway House***, I enjoyed making shorts under two minutes, but worried that they'd throw off the pacing when paired with shorts longer than ten minutes. ***Waxworks*** gave me the validation I needed. If this classic anthology did it, perhaps so could I.

DEAD OF NIGHT (FILM, 1945)

4 DIRECTORS | RUNTIME: 1HR 42MIN

-Notable Cast/Crew: Actor Mervyn Johns

-Wraparound type: Storytelling

-The setup: When an architect is invited to a bed & breakfast to help the owners rethink the way they utilize their space, he insists that his arrival there has been the subject of a recurring dream he's been having. Upon meeting a group of guests inside, he claims that they've been in these dreams as well. Some in the group believe him, but a skeptical psychiatrist obviously does not. One guest, a racecar driver, says that he's had similar experiences with inexplicable visions, and we transition to his story.

-First short: The racecar driver is about to board a bus, but then has a vision of a hearse, which scares him out of boarding. When the bus crashes soon after, he believes the vision saved his life.

-Return to wraparound: The guests begin going around the room, all telling stories of strange and spooky things that have happened to them. When the next guest goes into her story, the camera pushes past her, into a crackling fireplace as a segue device. It's a simple technique by today's standards, but one you'll see repeated over and over again in anthologies over the years. Someone had to do it first.

-Second short: The woman relays a chilling account of her experience with a ghost at a Christmas party.

-Return to wraparound: The guests continue going around the room as the psychiatrist attempts to debunk each one.

-Third short: A haunted mirror seeks to repeat the tragic deaths of its previous owners.

-Return to wraparound: The characters take solace in each other's stories, finding comfort in the fact that they're not the only ones who have had brushes with the paranormal.

-Fourth short: In this comedic short, the ghost of a golfer haunts his rival. It's interesting to note that the producers saved the funny short for the middle in an otherwise creepy anthology. Placing it here helps break the tension and add some variety to the tone.

-Return to wraparound: Here, ***Dead of Night*** breaks away from the humor of the fourth short and doubles down on the creepiness as we go to the psychiatrist's story.

-Fifth short: The psychiatrist tells of a legal case on which he was asked to consult. The case centers around a ventriloquist's dummy that allegedly has a mind of its own.

-Return to wraparound: Everything the architect foresaw in his dreams has so far come to fruition. Here, the anthology ventures into the surreal as he meanders through each short film's setting. Fairly abstract and mind bending, it ends in a style that would later be associated with the original ***Twilight Zone***. It feels like the anthology is folding in on itself. This technique would later be used in 2017's ***Ghost Stories***, as well as the season 1 finale to the 2019 ***Twilight Zone*** reboot.

-The takeaway: When referring to the first horror anthology film ever made, many people seem to skip over ***Unheimliche Geschichten*** and ***Waxworks***. 1945's ***Dead of Night*** gets much of the credit for being the first. Though it's incorrect, I understand why. It was the first "talkie" to utilize the Storytelling anthology format (***Unheimliche Geschichten*** and ***Waxworks*** were silent films). ***Dead of Night*** also has the distinction of providing a blueprint for many wonderful anthologies that would follow it. Andy Nyman, writer/director/producer/star of ***Ghost Stories***, even cites it as influential in our Section I interview.

ONE STEP BEYOND (SERIES, 1959-1961)

97 EPISODES | EPISODE RUNTIME: ~25MIN

-Notable Cast/Crew: Host John Newland

-Wraparound type: Horror Host

-The setup: Each episode opens with a voiceover from Newland: "What you're about to see is a matter of public record. Explain it, we cannot. Disprove it, we cannot. We simply invite you to explore with us, the amazing world of the unknown. To take that… one step beyond." Then, after an opening title sequence, he appears on camera in a scene that somehow corresponds to the story we're about to see. For example, in, "Night of April 14th," Newland introduces the story from the house in which it took place. This episode is about a woman who foresees the sinking of the Titanic just days before her trip on the ill-fated vessel. In "The Vision," Newland delivers an introduction in front of battlefield maps before transitioning to a tale about WWI troops transfixed by an unexplainable bright light shining down from the sky.

-A typical episode: In "The Dark Room," Newland points to a house's front door, saying that it's the scene of the crime which will be the episode's focus. In many episodes, the show transitions from the introduction to the main story with a simple cut, but this episode's segue is more complex than that. As Newland cryptically teases the audience about what terrible thing happened in this house, he begins to walk off camera. As he does so, he looks over his shoulder and down an alleyway, compelling the audience to follow his gaze. Just then, a car full of the story's main characters comes into view. As Newland leaves the scene, we are transported back into the past to learn what happened, and the whole transition happens in a single shot. Here, the primary method of transition from the introduction to the main story is an extremely clever blocking of the actors. In this tale, a woman living in this house is nearly killed by the ghost of a murderer who once lived there.

-Return to wraparound: After learning the truth and seeing the murderer's headstone, the woman walks off camera and Newland steps in for some closing remarks. This method of transition places the host within the narrative of the tale rather than outside of it, as so many horror hosts are forced to be.

-**The takeaway:** The trope of true paranormal stories dramatized with the aid of a host would later evolve with ***Unsolved Mysteries*** and again in the 2017 series, ***Lore***. Adapting a true paranormal story was something I had already done prior to watching ***One Step Beyond*** and its successors, but afterwards it became a thing I decided to embrace fully in ***Gravedigger Dave's Halfway House.***.

THE TWILIGHT ZONE (SERIES, 1959-1961)

156 EPISODES | EPISODE RUNTIME: VARIES FROM 25 TO 45MIN

TWILIGHT ZONE: THE MOVIE (FILM, 1983)

4 DIRECTORS | RUNTIME: 1HR 41MIN

THE TWILIGHT ZONE (SERIES, 1985-1989)

65 EPISODES | EPISODE RUNTIME: ~45MIN

ROD SERLING'S LOST CLASSICS (TV MOVIE, 1994)

1 DIRECTORS | RUNTIME: 1HR 29MIN

THE TWILIGHT ZONE (SERIES, 2002-2003)

43 EPISODES | EPISODE RUNTIME: ~45MIN

THE TWILIGHT ZONE (SERIES, 2019-CURRENT)

20 EPISODES | EPISODE RUNTIME: ~1HR

-Notable Cast/Crew: Hosts Rod Serling, Forest Whitaker, Jordan Peele, and too many talented actors to name

-Wraparound type: Horror Host

-The setup: The original ***Twilight Zone*** set the standard that most anthology filmmakers still strive for today. There were several variations of original host Rod Serling's introduction. My favorite was used for seasons four and five:

> You unlock this door with the key of imagination. Beyond it is another dimension—a dimension of sound, a dimension of sight, a dimension of mind. You're moving into a land of both shadow and substance, of things and ideas. You've just crossed over into the Twilight Zone.

This is always followed by some additional narration specific to each episode, and it's always filled with mystery and wonder. While many anthology hosts rely on gags and puns, Serling never does. The writing is deadly serious, and always impeccable.

-A typical episode: Of all the films and series I've analyzed in this book, ***Twilight Zone*** is definitely the most over-analyzed. I won't waste your time by going over the episodes that have already been dissected time and time again. In my opinion, the episodes of the original series that should be of greatest interest for anthology filmmakers are the ones that set up the potential for additional stories. Such episodes feel as though they could be wraparounds for their own anthologies if the producers had chosen to expand the concepts into standalone feature films. Perhaps they can serve as inspiration for modern anthology filmmakers.

A prime example is episode twelve of season four, "I Dream of Genie." When a man is offered a wish from a magic lamp, he pines over the possibilities. That concept could easily be translated into an anthology film's wraparound by taking the time to create a short film about each possible wish he imagines.

Similarly, the next episode, "The New Exhibit," shows a man who is driven mad by wax statues depicting famous murderers. At the beginning of this episode, we go on a tour of the wax museum in a scene that's reminiscent of the silent anthology film, ***Waxworks***, in which each statue serves as the subject of a short film. Fans of ***Black Mirror*** may also think of the episode "Black Museum" while watching this ***Twilight Zone*** episode.

Another episode that illustrates this point is the fourteenth episode of season three, "Five Characters in Search of an Exit." Like many ***Twilight Zone*** episodes it functions as a contained thriller. When five strange people inexplicably find themselves stuck in a white cylinder, they share stories about themselves and search for an escape. A setup such as this could be used as a springboard for an anthology filmmaker to launch into short films about each character's backstory. Of course, the twist ending of "Five Characters" would make short films about their lives impossible, but it's still a good jumping-off point.

-Return to wraparound: I mention in this book's introduction that I love stories that leave me with a sense of awe and dread. Serling was a master at that. This is his closing narration for, "The New Exhibit."

> The new exhibit became very popular at Marchand's, but of all the figures none was ever regarded with more dread than that of Martin Lombard Senescu. It was something about the eyes, people said. It's the look that one often gets after taking a quick walk through the Twilight Zone.

-The takeaway: If you don't believe me that the original series can be a good jumping-off point for the creation of more anthologies, just look at how many times the franchise has been revived (and at how good those revivals have been).

The 1983 theatrical film, ***Twilight Zone: The Movie***, was the first revival of the original series. It's also the only installment of the franchise that doesn't utilize a host to guide us through the stories. It simply relies on some opening narration and then follows a more tangential plot structure. It serves as a partial remake of original episodes, but also adds new content. The movie begins with an original sequence in which a hitchhiker, played by Dan Aykroyd, shows a friendly driver something, "really scary." In the next segment, which borrows from several original episodes, a racist man learns the true meaning of persecution as he travels through time and has run-ins with Nazis, the KKK, and American soldiers in the Vietnam War. The third segment stars Scatman Crothers, who is probably best known to horror fans for his role as Hallorann in ***The Shining***. In this magically-infused short, he travels to a nursing home to show the folks staying there how to be young again. This segment was directed by Steven Spielberg, and feels a bit like a proof-of-concept for his anthology series, ***Amazing Stories***. The fourth short, a remake of the classic episode, "It's a Good Life," is about a boy with telepathic powers who rules by fear to get whatever he wants. The fifth short is a remake of the classic episode, "Nightmare at 20,000 feet," which is a story I actually first became acquainted with through ***The Simpsons*** in "Treehouse of Horror IV." In this version, John Lithgow swears he sees a monster lurking on the wing of a commercial airline, though nobody else believes him. This anthology includes an epilogue, which brings back Aykroyd's character who, in an ambulance, asks Lithgow if he'd like to see something, "really scary," bringing the anthology full circle.

There was also an 80s revival TV series that followed in the wake of the movie's success. This series' long episode runtime allowed for multiple stories in each episode, though there were no overt attempts to connect those stories. That's not to say that the filmmakers involved weren't conscious of how an episode's segments would complement each other. In the DVD commentary for, "The Star," scribe Alan Brennert mentions how he modified Arthur C. Clark's original story to better fit the episode's other story. And in the commentary for "Quarantine," producer Phil DeGuere notes that the rural setting of both segments helped create cohesion. While it may seem natural to take these things under consideration, some anthology films suffer from the lack of cohesion that results when one doesn't.

Rod Serling's Lost Classics is a 1994 TV special that begins with a brief introduction by James Earl Jones. He tells viewers they're about to see two of Rod Serling's unproduced stories. The first is about a woman who, while at the cinema, sees her past, present, and future projected on the screen. Though no one else can see these images, she insists they're real, and obsessively attends screenings to learn more about her frightening future. The next is about a Civil War surgeon who travels to an island off the coast of Massachusetts, believing the residents are hoarding the secret to eternal life.

The 2002 revival series, though short-lived, represents a return to form with the inclusion of host Forest Whitaker. There's a time travel episode about an assasination attempt on an infant Adolf Hitler that's particularly chilling.

The 2019 reboot of the series, however, would be the iteration to most cleverly deconstruct and reinvent the role of the horror host. As defined in the introduction to Section II, a horror host breaks the fourth wall to address the audience directly. But in this series, a character in the season one finale, "Blurryman," actually senses the presence of the show's host when nobody else can. I don't want to spoil the episode, so I'll leave it at this: the episode is one of the most clever deconstructions of the anthology subgenre that I've ever seen, and asserts that Serling's campfire-style stories shouldn't be regarded as, "silly genre kid stuff."

Serling certainly wasn't exaggerating when he described, "a dimension as vast as space and as timeless as infinity." "Blurryman" takes it to the next level. Anthology filmmakers certainly have infinite knowledge to gain by examining how the original series has spawned (and will continue to spawn) such a plethora of great reboots.

• • •

13 DEMON STREET (SERIES, 1959-1960)

13 EPISODES | EPISODE RUNTIME: ~22MIN

-Notable Cast/Crew: Host Lon Chaney, Jr.

-Wraparound type: Horror Host

-The setup: Wind howls and lightning strikes as each episode opens with a shot of a creepy old building. While the opening credits roll over the house's number "13," the score helps us settle into the mood of the show. The host tells us that, as punishment for a heinous crime, he's been condemned to an eternity in this house. His task is to find a crime that's more repulsive than his own, at which point he'll be relieved of his punishment.

He invites the viewer to look with him upon a different grisly story in each episode. Sometimes he'll open a door, which is used to wipe to the episode's main story.

Other times he'll beckon the audience to follow him to a dark part of the house, allowing the segment to fade in through the darkness.

Conclusion: After creepy stories about bad people doing bad things, each episode ends with a return to the house where the man addresses the audience and says a final word. He never reveals exactly what crime he committed, but at each episode's conclusion we know that he still has more searching to do.

-The takeaway: Make sure you read the description and takeaway for the 1961 film, ***The Devil's Messenger***, for details on how unaired episodes of this show were re-framed to serve an entirely different narrative. This could give you insight into how multiple framing narratives could suit your shorts. Perhaps it'll help you realize that the first framing device you come up with isn't necessarily the *best* one you can come up with. As I found when developing ***Gravedigger Dave's Halfway House***, I came up with several wraparound concepts that simply didn't work before coming to the one that was ultimately used in the movie. It took me a long time, after many drafts, outlines, and treatments to find the right way to present my short films. I suggest you compare ***13 Demon Street*** to ***The Devil's Messenger***. It could help you realize that there's more than one wraparound concept that could frame your short films.

THE DEVIL'S MESSENGER (FILM, 1961)

2 DIRECTORS | RUNTIME: 1HR 12MIN

-Notable Cast/Crew: Actor Lon Chaney, Jr.

-Wraparound type: Thematic Throughline

-The setup: Opening credits roll as we descend into hell. People are lined up at the devil's desk, waiting for him to decide their final fate. A suicide victim approaches the desk, and the devil offers her a special position in hell as his messenger. Her first task is to deliver a special camera to a photographer who has not yet sinned, but is about to. The camera carries evil within it, and the devil tells his new messenger that he likes to make it easy for people up above to do what is required to join him down below.

-First short: The photographer wants to take a photo of a woman outside her house, but when she snubs him he murders her. But how will he react when pictures of the woman, which he swears he never took, keep on appearing in his portfolio?

-Return to wraparound: The devil defends his actions to the messenger, saying he only gives people the tools they require so that they may descend into evil, thus becoming his new recruits. Though reluctant to continue, the messenger agrees to deliver the next object, a pickaxe.

-Second short: A miner uses the pickaxe to discover the body of an ancient woman perfectly preserved in ice. He falls in love, believing her to still be alive. But how far will he go to protect this mysterious woman from the anthropologists who'd wish to study her?

-Return to wraparound: The devil gives the messenger a crystal ball, which he calls "the toy of the devil," because the people who use it only see what the devil lets them see. He promises her that if she delivers this final item, he'll bring her ex down to hell so that she can get even with him.

-Third short: A man goes to see a fortune teller, who tells him that he'll be dead at midnight, and that she'll be the one to take his life. While he eventually believes the prophecy to be true, he simply can't resist the urge to go to her to see how his final moments will play out.

-Return to wraparound: In hell now, the man from the third short is revealed to be the messenger's ex. The devil assigns them a task they must fulfill together; delivering an envelope containing information that could wipe out all of humanity. When they ask who they should deliver the envelope to, the devil breaks the fourth wall by pointing right to the camera, and saying, "them." The film concludes with shots of a nuclear holocaust. It is literal hell on earth.

-The takeaway: This anthology film is a repackaging of three unaired episodes of the TV show, ***13 Demon Street***, with a new frame story created to tie it all together. In this show, a condemned man (also played by Lon Chaney Jr.) is sentenced to search for a crime more heinous than his own. He is not to be released from the titular address until he does so. The fact that the shorts in ***The Devil's Messenger*** were initially intended to fit this wraparound highlights the versatility of horror shorts, as well as the malleability of frame stories. I took great solace upon this discovery as I struggled to develop a wraparound concept that would suit both the shorts I had already produced, as well as the ones I hoped to produce. I even finished, copyrighted and shelved a script called ***The Hooded Traveler***, which I hoped would serve as the glue for my short films. It was a relief to learn that other producers had found success in a similar endeavor. Don't be afraid to shelve an idea and continue working towards a better one.

• • •

TALES OF TERROR (1962)

1 DIRECTOR | RUNTIME: 1HR 29MIN

-Notable Cast/Crew: Director Roger Corman; Actor Vincent Price

-Wraparound type: Package Film, Thematic Throughline

-The setup: The film begins with the image of a beating heart as Vincent Price tells us to, "sit very still and listen." He asks, "Is your heart beating in this same rhythm?"

This opening has the effect of making a viewer immediately on-edge, more aware of their own heartbeat than they're probably used to. He says that this is the heartbeat of a dying man, and that this film's main concern is what happens during the process of death… and afterwards.

-First short: A woman who visits her father after twenty-six years of separation finds him overly hostile towards her. He reveals that he sent her away when she was only months old, as he blamed her for the death of her mother. While the father and daughter are able to make amends, the undead spirit of the mother uses their reunion as an opportunity to rise from the dead and seek revenge.

-Second short: We return to the beating heart, this time synced to the animated paw prints of a cat, as Price briefly introduces, "The Black Cat." In this second short, what starts as a slapstick comedy about a drunk competing with a connoisseur at a wine tasting turns dark and deadly when the drunk discovers his wife's affair. This adaptation, having been made 43 years after the version seen in ***Unheimliche Geschichten***, takes on a much more psychedelic and comedic quality.

-Third short: In this final short, "The Case of M. Valdemar," a dying man agrees to undergo an experiment in which his moment of death is sustained indefinitely, leaving him in a state of having a dead body but a living mind.

-The takeaway: There's something about Poe's work that is especially ripe for short film adaptation. ***Unheimliche Geschichten***, ***Tales of Terror***, ***Two Evil Eyes***, ***Extraordinary Tales***, and probably more have been directly inspired by his work. And guess what? His work is in the Public Domain, which means that you can adapt it too.

BLACK SABBATH (FILM, 1963)

1 DIRECTOR | RUNTIME: 1HR 32MIN

-Notable Cast/Crew: Actor Boris Karloff

-Wraparound type: Horror Host

The setup: This film features brief segues during which Boris Karloff, playing himself, gives the viewers a tongue-in-cheek introduction to each short.

-First short: A medical examiner is called to prepare a body during a midnight storm. When she steals a ring from the departed's finger, she's slowly driven mad by a nagging fly and then the sounds of dripping water around her house. When the corpse appears, it terrorizes her and forces her to choke herself. The ring is stolen again at the scene of the crime, leaving us to surmise that the cycle will continue.

-Return to wraparound: Karloff tells a cheeky joke about a haunted phone and pontificates about ghosts.

-Second short: A woman is terrorized by a man who won't stop calling her. He slips a letter under her door, which writes itself as she holds it in her hands. It signs itself, Frank, who she says is dead. She calls a friend, who comes over to comfort her and takes the phone off the hook. Frank sneaks in and strangles the friend. Then, the main character stabs Frank, killing him. But just as she thinks her torment is over, she hears Frank's voice coming from the telephone, telling her it's just begun.

-Return to wraparound: Karloff quips about vampires.

-Third short: This segment actually plays more like a fantasy movie than a horror movie. A horseman finds a slain bandit, and upon entering a nearby house in search of answers, learns that it is the patriarch of the house who's done the deed. All in the house urge the horseman to be on his way prior to the patriarch's return, but he's taken a liking to one of the daughters, and so he lingers against all warnings of bloodsucking and vampirism. The anthology ends here without returning to Karloff for any kind of epilogue.

-The takeaway: Lighthearted, jokey framing sequences are juxtaposed against darker, serious shorts. Each short has its own three act structure of sorts, but there's no attempt to build a cohesive narrative between the shorts and the framing device. Though the stories are all based on the work of a single author, Anton Chekhov, each short exists in isolation from the others both structurally and thematically. Without Karloff's presence between shorts, I'd have probably labeled this a Package Film anthology.

TWICE TOLD TALES (FILM, 1963)

1 DIRECTOR | RUNTIME: 2HR

-Notable Cast/Crew: Actor Vincent Price

-Wraparound type: Package Film

-The setup: This film opens by telling us we're in for "A Trio of Terror… Based on the famous Hawthorne Stories." It's of course Nathaniel Hawthorne's work that's being adapted in this movie. Hawthorne's original book, ***Twice Told Tales***, collected stories that had already been published, hence their being "twice told." After the opening credits, the camera zooms in on the hands of a skeleton opening a book to a page that reads, "Dr. Heidegger's Experiment."

-First short: In this tale, a man and an old friend discover his fiance's remains perfectly preserved thirty-eight years after her death. They determine her youthful appearance to be the result of a stream of water leaking into her casket; a fountain of youth. When each man drinks from the fountain they find their youth restored, and conduct an experiment which brings the fiance back from the dead. But with these three reunited, old secrets come back to haunt them.

-Return to wraparound: We cut back to the skeleton's hands as they turn the book to a new title page reading, "Rappaccini's Daughter."

-Second short: When a man falls in love with his next door neighbor's daughter, he learns that they and their garden have something sinister to hide. (Side note: though this segment is based on a Hawthorne short story, it was not included in the original book, ***Twice Told Tales***.)

-Return to wraparound: At the conclusion of this segment the skeleton hand turns the page once more, this time to "The House of the Seven Gables."

-Third short: In the final segment of this anthology, a man and his wife travel to his family's home in search of a vault allegedly hidden there. Witchcraft, generational curses, and bleeding walls set the stage for this paranormal conspiracy. This segment wasn't adapted from a short story, but rather from Hawthorne's novel of the same name.

• • •

KWAIDAN (FILM, 1964)

1 DIRECTOR | RUNTIME: 3HR 3MIN

-Notable Cast/Crew: Director Masaki Kobayashi

-Wraparound type: Package Film

-The setup: This anthology, set in feudal Japan, opens with luscious shots of food coloring descending into water as credits roll. In the special features of this film's DVD, the director discusses how this was the first film he'd shot in color. In this opening credit sequence, you can clearly see that he's enjoying the experimentation.

-First short: A young samurai leaves his first wife for a rich noblewoman, only to deeply regret his choices. Years later, when he returns to his first wife, he finds her waiting for him, just as he'd always imagined her. But why hasn't she aged, and why is she so forgiving of him? He'll soon learn she's harboring a dark secret.

-Second short: Men seeking refuge in a hut are haunted by the ghost of a woman. After she drains the life out of the older man, she decides to spare the younger, but she makes him promise not to ever speak of these events, otherwise she'll return and kill him. The young man goes on to marry and start a family, but his past with the ghost eventually comes back to haunt him. For an update on this story, see the third short in ***Tales From the Darkside: The Movie***.

-Third short: A musician's songs bring back the ghost of a fallen warrior. The evolution of this story relies heavily on the aid of a narrator, who goes through the history of the war in which the ghost fought.

-Fourth short: A man is disturbed when he sees a face other than his own reflected in a cup of tea. No matter how many times he dumps it out and refills it, the mysterious face is still there. Is the tea-drinker being haunted, or simply losing his mind?

-The takeaway: In the special features of this film's DVD, assistant director Kiyoshi Ogasawara says of the film's director, "He'd flip through the [art] books looking for tonalities and color schemes to use in the four stories in ***Kwaidan***...The ones he liked he'd cut out with scissors and glue into a scrapbook. So the first story would have this tonality, the second would have this color scheme... The goal was to keep the tonalities in balance."

In this way, the filmmakers set about giving each story a distinct look, and they were extremely successful in this endeavor. So be sure to take inspiration from wherever you can, especially from sources outside of the horror genre. This'll broaden your horizons and help make sure that your shorts don't feel like copies of other short films.

• • •

DR. TERROR'S HOUSE OF HORRORS (FILM, 1965)

1 DIRECTOR | RUNTIME: 1HR 38MIN

-Notable Cast/Crew: Amicus Productions; Actors Peter Cushing, Donald Sutherland, & Michael Gough

-Wraparound type: Mind's Eye

-The setup: The film begins with six men cramming into a seating compartment on a train. The eldest of the group, Dr. Terror, drops his bag, sending a deck of tarot cards, amongst other items, spilling out. When the other passengers question their purpose, Dr. Terror reveals their ability to predict the future, and calls them his, "house of horrors." He invites one of them to tap the deck three times so that he can draw a card and reveal their fortune. When the first volunteer does so, we transition to the first short.

-First short: This man has a vision that he travels back to his family's old home to assist with a renovation. While there, he discovers a legendary werewolf's coffin hidden in its walls, as well as the true reason his presence was requested.

-Return to wraparound: Transitioning back to the train, it turns out this man is currently on his way to the family home depicted in the first short, and is stirred by his fortune. But his fate isn't sealed, as the card's prediction is not a matter of certainty, but only a possibility.

There is one naysayer in the traincar who continues to doubt the doctor's prowess, but another man nevertheless volunteers to learn his fortune. This man is on the train to meet his family for a vacation. Dr. Terror's prediction begins as they return home from their trip.

-Second short: The man's wife notices a vine growing on the side of the house that hadn't been there when they'd left. When they try to cut the vine, it aggressively fights back. They hire a biologist to investigate the plant, who says without irony, "A plant like that could take over the world." It's campy, but great.

-Return to wraparound: On the train, Dr. Terror draws another card, hoping it will contain information on how this man can avoid the homicidal vine, but isn't happy with the results and avoids revealing it to his co-passengers. When another man volunteers to be next, cards are drawn and we transition to the next short.

-Third short: We learn that this man plays a trumpet in a jazz band that's been booked to tour in the Caribbean. When he seeks to exploit the region's religious traditions, bad luck seems to follow him everywhere he goes.

-Return to wraparound: On the train, the naysayer continues to doubt the doctor's ability to tell the future, but is nevertheless goaded into having his own fortune read.

-Fourth short: The naysayer is a snobby art critic engaged in a comical feud with an artist played by Michael Gough (an actor perhaps best known for playing Batman's butler, Alfred). When the critic lashes out violently against the artist, leading to the amputation of the artist's hand, the severed appendage begins stalking the critic, and it will get its revenge in the most ironic of ways.

-Return to wraparound: Despite having been the naysayer of the group, the critic is shook to the core when Doctor Terror finishes telling his story. Finally, the last train passenger, played by Donald Sutherland, has his fortune told.

-Fifth short: When this character, a newly wed, begins to believe his wife is a vampire, he's torn over whether to kill her or let her continue sucking the blood of a local child.

-Return to wraparound: In the final moments of the film, Dr. Terror is confronted about his identity. His reply: "Have you not guessed?"

-The takeaway: Like ***Unheimliche Geschichten***, this film required the main actors from the shorts to star in the frame stories as well. While this technique would later be used in the Amicus anthology, ***Asylum***, it is actually not a common technique in anthology filmmaking, primarily for logistical reasons.

In the 2016 film, ***Patient Seven***, older actors were hired for the shooting of the frame story so they could relay the deeds of their younger selves. This made a lot of sense, production wise, for this film, as each short was shot by a different director, in some cases years before the release of the anthology. In the case of ***Dr. Terror's House of Horrors***, however, the production of each segment under the guise of a single director made this gathering of actors for the frame story more feasible.

Keep all of this in mind as you set out on your journey. Will you be gathering shorts from different directors made over a wide span of time? If so, you probably don't want to write a wraparound that requires you rehire the actors from each short. If, however, you're shooting the whole anthology in a single window of time, perhaps emulating this aspect of ***Dr. Terror's House of Horrors*** will make sense.

TORTURE GARDEN (FILM, 1965)

1 DIRECTOR | RUNTIME: 1HR 38MIN

-Notable Cast/Crew: Amicus Productions; Actors Burgess Meredith, Jack Palance, & Peter Cushing

-Wraparound type: Mind's Eye

-The setup: Dr. Diablo, the curator of a carnival sideshow about execution and torture, invites a small group of fairgoers to spend a few extra bucks to see an exhibit of true horror. He says, "If you can gain a knowledge of your inner evil, then you will have been forewarned, and you perhaps can escape the monstrous act and the hideous consequences."

The most striking feature of this strange exhibit is a wax figure holding thread and shears; the thread representing human lives, and the shears representing their bitter end. Diablo invites one patron to gaze into shears to see his possible future. (Be sure to look for a guest appearance by the wax woman in each short, either in the flesh or in the form of a portrait.)

-First short: This first man, a greedy nephew, plots to murder his uncle to secure the family inheritance for himself.

-Return to wraparound: Diablo invites the next patron to gaze at the shears.

-Second short: A woman goes to disturbing lengths to achieve fame and notoriety.

-Return to wraparound: Diablo invites the next patron to gaze at the shears.

-Third short: The only thing standing between a woman and her true love is a piano possessed with the spirit of his domineering mother. (It's interesting to note here that all of the shorts were penned by the writer of ***Psycho***.)

-Return to wraparound: Diablo invites the next patron to gaze at the shears.

-Fourth short: A budding relationship between two Poe aficionados leads to the startling revelation that the legendary poet may not be resting in peace after all.

-Return to wraparound: As the fifth patron readies to hear his fortune, he suddenly turns on Diablo. As we think we're about to see a fifth short, this anthology takes a very unexpected turn, and ends with a twist that I won't spoil here.

-The takeaway: ***Torture Garden***'s first short employs a very clever technique to show the passage of time. In one shot, we see a closeup of our main character, surveying a house with his eyes for a hidden fortune. We then cut to a shot of the house, presumably from his point of view, but then the camera pans over to show him already deep into his search. The same technique is used again later in the short. In the cellar, he finds a patch of dirt. The next cut shows a closeup of a lit candle. When the camera zooms out, we see that he's already dug a deep hole in search of the fortune.

These techniques are simple. They don't require a timelapse, a shot of a clock, text, or a dissolve to convey the passage of time. They zip from the character's decision to act right to his work already in progress. Short filmmakers should take notice of techniques such as these. One of the shorts in my film, ***Gravedigger Dave's Halfway House*** dissolves to black several times to show the passage of a day. I wish I would've found a more graceful way to accomplish that.

1970s - 1980s

THE HOUSE THAT DRIPPED BLOOD (FILM, 1971)

1 DIRECTOR | RUNTIME: 1HR 42MIN

-Notable Cast/Crew: Amicus Productions; Actors Peter Cushing & Christopher Lee

-Wraparound type: Storytelling

-The setup: The frame story begins with an investigator arriving at an ornate mansion in search of a missing actor. An officer tells him of other strange incidents that have occurred there as we transition to the short films.

-First short: A writer staying at the house fears he is going mad when he begins seeing one of his characters around the property. The writer's psychiatrist tells him, "an author's characters are extensions of his own personality, sometimes the part of it that he normally tries to conceal from himself." Is the writer's vision evidence of an alternate personality, or is there something even more diabolical afoot?

-Return to wraparound: The officer blames the incident not on the people involved, but on the house itself. He then tells the tale of the next tennant, a retired stockbroker.

-Second short: The stockbroker, a lonely man played by the legendary Peter Cushing, seems to be longing for a woman from his past, and is shocked to find a figure bearing her distinct likeness when visiting a local wax museum. What dark secret is the museum's curator hiding?

-Return to wraparound: Again the officer insists that the grim fates of all of the tenants are caused by the evil house. The inspector then pays a visit to the owner of the house, who tells the story of the next man to rent it.

-Third short: When this man, a father played by Christopher Lee, moves in he immediately hires a full time tutor for his daughter. As the tutor learns of the true nature of the father and daughter's relationship, will she be able to save them from each other?

-Return to wraparound: The house's owner insists that these events were caused by the house itself, not the people staying in it. He then tells the inspector the story of the missing actor.

-Fourth short: While shooting a vampire film, the actor temporarily stays at the house. He finds a cloak at a local shop, which he intends to use as a prop, until the cloak starts bringing out the vampire within him.

-Return to wraparound: The inspector gets the keys from the owner and, against all warnings, goes to the house in search of clues. In the cellar, he discovers that the vampires he was just told about are in fact real, and that he must fight to the death if he hopes to escape. In the final shot of the film, the owner steps in and breaks the fourth wall, encouraging the viewer to rent the house, and then walks off.

-The takeaway: The makers of this film, and most other Amicus anthologies, would be unable to solicit films from the public, as I did with ***Gravedigger Dave Meets His Match***. This is because ***The House that Dripped Blood*** requires the same location be used in each short as in the wraparound. Such a choice makes things logistically complicated and should be considered when developing your concept. Producing a wraparound AND each short film in the same location might make your production more like a typical feature than an anthology in certain respects.

• • •

TALES FROM THE CRYPT (FILM, 1972)

1 DIRECTOR | RUNTIME: 1HR 32MIN

-Notable Cast/Crew: Amicus Productions; Actor Peter Cushing

-Wraparound type: Mind's Eye

-The setup: This film begins with a tour guide leading a group through ancient catacombs. When four men and a woman get separated from the official tour, they enter a room while in search of the larger group. In this room they meet a man clothed in a brown robe as the door seals itself behind them. This Crypt Keeper asks the woman what drew her to the catacombs and what her plans were for after the tour.

-First short: We see the woman murder her husband on Christmas Eve. In one very busy night, she has to hide his body from their young daughter, and defend her house from a deranged murderer dressed as Santa Claus. All the while, she listens to Christmas music on the radio, giving the segment an extremely creepy feel. This short is off-the-walls bonkers.

-Return to wraparound: The woman is about to say that she has no intentions of murdering her husband, when The Crypt Keeper cuts her off and moves on to the next person. This man says that he's planning on going home to his wife after the tour, as we dissolve to the next short.

-Second short: The man leaves his wife and daughter to elope with his mistress. Unfortunately for him, he falls asleep at the wheel and they get into a horrible accident. When he stumbles out to look for the mistress, people run from him in horror. Finally seeing his reflection, he learns that he's a walking corpse, and that he actually died in the crash. But then, just as he learns this, he wakes up in the car with his mistress. It was all a bad dream. At least, this is what he thinks until they get into the same exact car wreck. He is stuck in a loop, damned to experience the same horrible events over and over again.

-Return to wraparound: The Crypt Keeper reveals his purpose. He says that he wants to show a thing that each one of them is capable of doing. The third man says that he doesn't want to know, but The Crypt Keeper says that he must.

-Third short: In an attempt to get his neighbor to move away, this man conducts a maniacal plan to ruin his life. But instead of the neighbor moving away, he instead kills himself, leaving our main character with a whole new set of problems to fix.

-Return to wraparound: With a great amount of guilt, he admits that he never liked this neighbor of his, as The Crypt Keeper turns his attention to the fourth person.

-Fourth short: This man is going broke, and he and his wife decide to use an ancient statue that allegedly grants wishes. Things go horribly wrong, as they inevitably do with horror stories involving wishes, but this version of the trope is particularly haunting.

-**Return to wraparound:** It becomes clear after the fourth short that the members of the group are unable to see each other's fortunes. Each person can only see their own fortune, not the fortunes of the others in the catacomb. The Crypt Keeper tells the final person that he hopes they're all able to learn from what they see.

-Fifth short: This man takes up a job as the superintendent at a home for the blind. But when he mistreats the residents, they plot a revenge that involves a hungry dog, a tight maze, and a lot of razor blades. It actually feels somewhat like a precursor to ***Saw*** in its final moments.

-**Return to wraparound:** The Crypt Keeper finally allows them to leave. But when the door they came through opens, it doesn't lead back the way they came, but to a blinding white light. The Crypt Keeper tells them that he was actually showing them the reason they are stuck in the catacomb for all eternity. He asks, "Who's next." Then, in a final moment similar to ***The Devil's Messenger***, he breaks the fourth wall and says, "Perhaps you."

-The takeaway: This film was made over fifteen years prior to the HBO version of the franchise featuring the beloved skeletal Cryptkeeper, but is likewise inspired by the same EC Comics. On the surface, this Crypt Keeper appears to be a living human rather than an undead monster. They're similar name and function, but much different in demeanor. Nevertheless, fans of the beloved HBO franchise should definitely give this film a watch.

• • •

ASYLUM (FILM, 1972)

1 DIRECTOR | RUNTIME: 1 HR 28 MIN

-Notable Cast/Crew: Amicus Productions; Actor Peter Cushing; Director Roy Ward Baker

-Wraparound type: Storytelling

-The setup: A young psychologist arrives at an asylum to interview for a job and is given a challenge to prove his talent to the man in charge. To do so, he must determine which of the patients ran the asylum before going mad a few days prior. Our protagonist ascends the stairs and goes about interviewing several patients. He meets the first one in her room, and she agrees to tell her tale.

-First short: The first patient was having a affair with a married man who agrees to murder his wife so they can run away together. He chops his wife into several pieces and becomes wary of a strange piece of jewelry she owns, deciding to keep it with her dismembered corpse. But what will he do with that jewelry when it causes her body to reanimate?

-Return to wraparound: An orderly brings our protagonist to meet the second patient, who had a career as a tailor.

-Second short: A customer asks the tailor to make a suit for his son using a strange material and following a specific set of instructions that include tailoring only after midnight. When he delivers the suit, the tailor discovers that the customer has no money to pay for the suit, and that the son's corpse is being stored in his house. What morbid intentions does the customer have?

-Return to wraparound: The third patient tells our protagonist that she has a background in medicine as she begins to tell her story.

-Third short: The third patient returns home from a treatment program to learn that her brother has hired a nurse to watch over her. He also forbids her from mentioning a woman named Lucy, and we begin to get hints that this Lucy may be a figment of her imagination. When the stabbing starts, will people believe that Lucy is to blame?

-Return to wraparound: The fourth patient doesn't tell the story of how he got to the asylum, thus there's no flashback. He instead tells our protagonist of the dolls he's building and how he plans to transfer his consciousness to one that bears his likeness. Believing he's solved the mystery of who formerly ran the asylum, our protagonist rushes to tell an orderly. But things are more than they seem in this madhouse.

In the epilogue, another young psychiatrist arrives for an interview and is greeted at the door by the orderly, implying the cycle will continue.

-The takeaway: The plot of this anthology never slows down, as each short adds to the mystery established in the wraparound. All information we learn during the flashbacks is information learned by the protagonist, which he can possibly use to achieve his goal of determining which of the patients formerly ran the asylum. This means that every flashback is propelling the plot of the frame story forward instead of slowing it down, as with some anthology films. In this way, ***Asylum*** forces the audience to problem-solve with the protagonist during the flashbacks, making the viewing of the film an active experience.

While watching this film, I found the unreliable narrators to be particularly inspiring. And after pondering for at least a month over how I might be able to introduce such tension to ***Gravedigger Dave's Halfway House***, I finally stumbled upon an answer. By the time I'd watched ***Asylum*** I had already made five shorts, one of which was a true ghost story. My way to apply what I'd learned from

Asylum would be to give a character, and thus the audience, the task of deducing which tales told by Gravedigger Dave were true, and which were made up. This would become the crux of all of my marketing, and it was directly inspired by ***Asylum***.

• • •

THE VAULT OF HORROR (FILM, 1973)

1 DIRECTOR | RUNTIME: 1HR 27MIN

-Notable Cast/Crew: Amicus Productions; Director Roy Ward Baker

-Wraparound type: Storytelling

-The Setup: This anthology begins with five men entering an elevator one by one. It brings them to a sub-basement, even though two of them say they pushed the button for the ground floor. When the doors open, they're let into an ornate room with a table that's been set for five. They sit, all agreeing that it feels like they're in a dream. Even the cinematography takes on a dreamlike quality. Pouring drinks, one of the men tells the others about a dream he had that felt all too real to him.

-First short: This man tracks down his sister with the intention of murdering her over their father's fortune, only to have the tables turned on him when he learns she's part of a society of vampires.

-Return to wraparound: This first man seems confused by his dream, and claims to not even have a sister. As the second man describes his dream, we transition to the next short.

-Second short: He grows increasingly frustrated with his new wife. It seems she's unable to keep his house exactly as he likes it. Over time he wears her down psychologically until she murders him with a hammer and neatly organizes his remains in jars, as if canning veggies for the winter.

-Return to wraparound: The second man exclaims how real the dream felt, as the third man goes into a description of his dream.

-Third short: While traveling in India in search of a new magic trick for his act, he meets a real magician who wields real magic. But when she refuses to sell him her trick, he goes to desperate measures to steal it from her. Of course, his greed backfires on him.

-Return to wraparound: All of the men are apparently afraid that the evil lurking in their subconscious is perhaps revealing their true nature. The fourth man goes into a description of his vision.

-Fourth short: He fakes his own death with the help of a friend so the two can split the insurance money. Like the previous short, their greed turns out to be their downfall.

-Return to wraparound: An artist tells his story,

-Fifth Short: We learn that a spell has been cast over him, making it so that anything he does to a portrait happens to that person in real life. He uses this new-found ability to take revenge against three men who have wronged him. But, as is the case with many a horror short, things ultimately backfire on him.

-**Return to wraparound:** This film ends as you may have expected if you're an Amicus fan. It turns the five men are in a purgatorial state, forced to tell the tales of their evil deeds over and over again, for all eternity. Like ***Tales From the Crypt***, this film shows us segments which at first seem like predictions of a possible future, when they are instead events that have already come to pass.

-**The takeaway:** In true Amicus fashion, the film invites you to look for clues in the dreams. Why have these men been brought to this place and what do their dreams have to do with it? We become active participants in the solving of this riddle.

Another takeaway is to take little bits of inspiration wherever you can find them. It may seem like a small thing (it is a small thing) but while watching this movie I had a flash of inspiration in regards to my title screen for ***Gravedigger Dave's Halfway House***. I thought it'd be interesting to include the copyright info you used to see on the title screens of 70s films. So, I included a bit of fine print beneath my title: "Copyright MMXIX, All Rights Reserved." I also included my Hexagon Motion Pictures logo in place of the MPAA logo. Again, it probably seems like an insignificant thing to latch onto, but these elements help set a certain mood and hopefully create a sense of association between my anthology and the horror films of the 70s.

TRILOGY OF TERROR (FILM, 1975)

1 DIRECTOR | RUNTIME: 1HR 12MIN

-Notable Cast/Crew: Director Dan Curtis

-Wraparound type: Package Film, Thematic Throughline

-The setup: This anthology features three short films with no wraparound, but all three star the same actress, Karen Black, playing a different character. Additionally, all are based on short stories by Richard Matheson. With the lack of any sort of framing device, the film relies on text to navigate from segment to segment. All three segment titles include the name of that segment's main character, helping drive home the theme of the consistent actress in all shorts.

-First short: "Julie," starts with a student who becomes infatuated with his teacher, Julie. On a date, he drugs her and photographs her while she's unconscious. But as their twisted relationship progresses, she reveals that it's he who has been manipulated.

-Second short: "Millicent and Therese," features feuding twin sisters, each of whom insists that the other is evil incarnate. It's apparent early on, however, that the two characters will not share a single scene together. Are they the same person, or is the filmmaker toying with his audience?

-Third short: "Amelia," is about a woman who buys an old warrior doll as a gift for her anthropologist boyfriend. A scroll that came with the doll reads that if the gold chain is removed from the doll's neck, a warrior's spirit will merge with the doll and it'll come to life. Inevitably, the chain falls off the doll and mayhem ensues.

-The takeaway: Director Dan Curtis would take a similar approach with a recurring actress in the 1996 sequel, ***Trilogy of Terror II***. The 2008 animated package film, ***Batman: Gotham Knight*** would likewise do the same with voice actor Kevin Conroy. Intended to bridge the gap between ***Batman Begins*** and ***The Dark Knight***, this package includes several shorts with wildly different animation styles. But the consistent voice for Batman helps maintain a level of cohesion between each story. Consider a way you might be able to similarly create cohesion between your short films. It doesn't have to be an actor, though. Perhaps it's a recurring prop, location, or even a recurring musical theme. There are many ways to create a throughline within your anthology.

THE UNCANNY (FILM, 1977)

1 DIRECTOR | RUNTIME: 1HR 29MIN

-Notable Cast/Crew: Actors Peter Cushing & Donald Pleasence

-Wraparound type: Storytelling

-The setup: The film begins with opening credits over strange paintings of cats. We join an author, played by Peter Cushing, who leaves his home to visit the home of a publisher interested in his work. Along the way he seems to be stalked by cats who watch his every move. Cushing believes cats are demonic in nature, and wants to tell the world. First he must convince the publisher. He shows the publisher a police report as we transition to the first short.

-First short: When an old woman revises her will, writing her greedy nephew out of it, he and the old woman's house keeper plan a horrible plot against her. But when the old woman's 10+ cats get involved, their plan goes off the rails.

-Return to wraparound: The publisher isn't convinced, saying the cats only chewed at the victim's bodies because they were starving. Cushing doesn't challenge his logic, but instead goes into another story.

-**Second short**: An orphan goes to live with her wicked aunt and cousin. When her adoptive family threatens the orphan's cat, they'll use witchcraft to defend themselves. This short features some exceptionally clever trick photography that feels like something of a precursor to ***Honey, I Shrunk the Kids***.

-Return to wraparound: Cushing is petrified of the publisher's cat, remarking that the pet is spying on them to make sure they behave. Each time we return to these wraparound segments he seems increasingly paranoid.

-Third short: When an actress is murdered on-set by her husband and his mistress, the actress' cat will seek its revenge by tampering with the film studio's dangerous props.

-Return to wraparound: Cushing's character claims that cats have been "exploiting the human race for centuries." As Cushing departs, the publisher's cat has its own ideas about what will become of the proposed manuscript.

-The takeaway: While this film is often mistaken for an Amicus anthology, its wraparound actually lacks the dramatic tension that Amicus films usually have. There seems to be no mystery to solve in ***The Uncanny***'s wraparound. One character has a point to prove, and the other refuses to believe it. At their best, Amicus wraparounds are more complex than this.

THE MONSTER CLUB (FILM, 1981)

1 DIRECTOR | RUNTIME: 1HR 44MIN

-Notable Cast/Crew: Director Roy Ward Baker; Actors John Carradine & Vincent Price

-Wraparound types: Storytelling, Film Within a Film

-The setup: The anthology begins with real world horror author R. Chetwynd Hayes, played by John Carradine, being attacked by a vampire played by Vincent Price. The vampire drinks some of Hayes' blood, but not enough to kill him. In return for his blood, the vampire offers to bring Hayes, of whose horror stories the vampire is a huge fan, to the Monster Club, a place where all manner of ghouls can have a drink in peace. The vampire promises that he and his monster friends will supply him with ample material for future stories. At the club, we transition to the shorts.

-First short: The vampire tells Hayes the story of Shadmock, a humanoid monster whose harsh, shrieking whistle causes various disfigurements to all who hear it. When a woman and her boyfriend attempt to steal from him, their plans backfire with terrible consequences.

-Return to wraparound: Back in the club, a band performs a punny song about a vampire being, "a sucker for love." Afterwards, a "vampire film producer" is invited to the stage. He projects a film onto a small screen and explains that it's autobiographical, as we watch with him. This marks a shift in the storytelling-style that had been established in the transition to the first short. We're now in Film Within a Film territory.

-Second short: In the vampire producer's coming-of-age biopic, he's bullied for being odd, but doesn't know why he's odd. It all comes into focus however, when he learns that his father is being pursued by vampire hunters. If he is to save himself and his family, the father must outsmart his hunters, and show his son what it means to be a vampire in a world that fears them.

-Return to wraparound: A curtain is drawn over the movie screen and the crowd applauds. The party resumes as another band takes the stage to play a song that features a pole dance by an undead skeleton. No joke. Afterwards, the vampire has another story for Hayes.

-Third short: A horror movie director travels to a remote town to scout locations for his next project, only to discover that it's inhabited by flesh-eating ghouls who thwart his every attempt to escape.

-Return to wraparound: The vampire nominates Hayes to be inducted into the club, his justification being that humans are the most vile creatures of all. After some debate, the monsters invite him as an official member and celebrate with a dance to the official Monster Club song. This isn't the only anthology of this era that features dance parties that feel totally separate from the rest of the film. Apparently, it was an 80s thing, as we'll also see in 1985's ***Night Train to Terror***.

-The Takeaway: There's a meta narrative at work in this frame story, as all of the short films within this anthology were written by the real Hayes. Thus, the film's premise is that Hayes only learned about these stories because of the events depicted in the wraparound. The 1993 anthology, ***The Necronomicon***, takes a similar approach in adapting H.P. Lovecraft's short stories.

• • •

CREEPSHOW (FILM, 1982)

1 DIRECTOR | RUNTIME: 2HR

CREEPSHOW 2 (FILM, 1987)

1 DIRECTOR | RUNTIME: 1HR 32MIN

CREEPSHOW (SERIES, 2019-CURRENT)

7 EPISODES | EPISODE RUNTIME: ~45MIN

-Notable Cast/Crew: Director George A. Romero; Writer Stephen King; Actors Adrienne Barbeau, Leslie Neilsen, & Ted Danson

-Wraparound types: Thematic Throughline, Tangential Throughline, Horror Host

-The setup: ***Creepshow*** begins outside the house of a boy named Billy. We hear that inside his father is yelling at him for reading a trashy ***Creepshow*** comic. After the abusive father tosses the mag in the trash can outside, Billy heads to bed. But he smiles when he sees that the comic's ghastly host, The Creep, has come to life and is floating outside his bedroom window. The Creep flies down to the garbage and opens up the discarded comic, showing us what's inside as we transition through a comic book panel into the first short.

-First short: On the anniversary of his murder (which also happens to be Father's Day) an insufferable patriarch will rise from the dead and take revenge on the family that betrayed him.

-Return to wraparound: The Creep turns the page of the comic, bringing us to the next short.

-Second short: A dimwitted farmer, played by Stephen King, finds a meteor in his backyard. But his dreams of profit will be squelched by the meteor's aggressively invasive properties, as it quickly transforms him into a plant-monstrosity.

-Return to wraparound: As The Creep turns to the next story, I couldn't help but notice the appearance of ads. Comic book fans familiar with the style of ads that appeared in 60s comics will quickly notice how spot-on they are to the time period. Whether this is done simply for nostalgia's sake, or rather has some importance to the plot remains to be seen.

-Third short: ***Creepshow***'s comedic irony rises to its plateau, as its most dramatically intense short features its most comedic actors: Leslie Neilsen and Ted Danson. Here, the choice to cast against-type is done with great effect. When Neilsen discovers that his wife is having an affair with Danson, he buries Danson neck deep in the sand so that the incoming tide will kill him.

-Return to wraparound: The Creep turns a page.

-Fourth short: When a university custodian finds an old crate hidden in an air duct, the ape-like monster trapped inside will not only wreak havoc on the faculty, but also bring out the professor's dark side.

-Return to wraparound: The Creep turns a page.

-Fifth short: A cruel businessman gets exactly what he deserves when an overwhelming horde of roaches invade his apartment

-Return to wraparound: The importance of the ads we've been seeing in the comic book is finally revealed. It's the morning now, and two garbage men find the comic on the ground and begin flipping through it out of curiosity. They chat about the ads and notice that someone has already sent away for a voodoo doll that is advertised in the book. In the final moment of ***Creepshow***, we see the comic's original owner, Billy, with said voodoo doll, repaying his father for years of abuse (and hatred of comic books).

-The takeaway: ***Creepshow*** has clearly been influenced by the horror comics published by EC Comics, like ***Tales from the Crypt***, and it's title font takes influence from Warren Publishing's ***Creepy*** comic book series. Combine that with The Creep's appearance and the overall tone of the stories, it almost seems as though King and Romero would've liked to have used the ***Creepy*** branding. Perhaps they were unable to obtain the rights to ***Creepy*** for their films, so they created the branding of ***Creepshow*** instead. However it came about, they made a film that is a perfect homage to some of the greatest comics ever written.

-The sequel's setup: While the first installment of the franchise resides firmly in Thematic Throughline territory, the sequel begins to venture into what I call a Tangential plot structure. ***Creepshow 2*** is again based on stories written by Stephen King. The wraparound begins with a delivery truck rolling into a small New England town. The delivery man (The Creep in disguise) tosses a load of packages out the back, which are eagerly unwrapped by Billy. Here, the frame story transitions from live action to animation as Billy finds the latest issue of a ***Creepshow*** comic book, the cover of which depicts the final scene from the first ***Creepshow*** film. As he opens the comic to take a look, scenes from the forthcoming shorts are depicted in the comic's panels as opening credits roll overtop.

With a lightning strike, we transition to an old stone mansion where an animated Creep says that the audience must be "gluttons for PUNishment if they're back for more." He grabs a comic and waves it towards the audience as we transition to live action.

-First short: A shop owner and his wife are robbed and terrorized by three thugs at gunpoint. But when the old Native American statue that's posted outside comes to life and intervenes, things go haywire for the three thugs.

-Return to wraparound: The last frame of this first short dissolves to an illustrated comic book panel, bringing us back to the frame story. Billy (animated) goes to the post office to pick up the seeds for a venus fly trap that he's ordered from an ad in his comic. As he walks off camera, The Creep pops up from behind the counter and makes good on his promise to be punny, bringing us to the next short. Again, The Creep holds up a ***Creepshow*** comic so that one panel will take up the whole screen, allowing the filmmakers to seamlessly dissolve from animation to live action.

-Second short: Four college students travel to a lake where they swim to a dock, only to be picked off one by one by a living oil slick.

-Return to wraparound: Billy (animated) finishes this section of his comic as The Creep makes some punny jokes about the oil slick. Some bullies chase Billy down and squash the plant he just picked up from the post office. And just as Billy escapes, The Creep transitions to one last story.

-Third short: A self-absorbed woman commits a hit and run. But when the corpse continues to haunt her as she tries to make her getaway, she'll go to increasingly extreme measures to make sure he stays dead. This short is a great example of King's over-the-top brand of horror comedy.

-Return to wraparound: The Creep speaks from inside a comic book panel and advises readers not to pick up hitchhikers… "on the hood of your car." We then go back to Billy's story as he defeats the bullies with the help of the giant venus flytraps from the comic book ad, until finally dissolving back to the initial live action frame story, in which The Creep tosses comic books out of the back of a box truck as credits roll.

-The takeaway: This anthology features a frame story within a frame story. It begins with a live action setup that transitions to an animated wraparound, which later concludes with a return to live action. Compounding on this Tangential Throughline, The Creep exists in three planes of storytelling. He's in live action, distributing comic books. Then, as the film transitions to animation, he exists both within and outside of Billy's comic book. This makes him truly omniscient within this universe, able to observe the shorts both as an outsider and as a participant.

There was a third installment in the official film series, but it feels related to the first two in name only as it totally eschews the comic book aesthetic. However this franchise got another opportunity to live on in the form of a TV series that began in 2019.

Like several of the ***Twilight Zone*** revivals over the years, the 2019 ***Creepshow*** series manages to honor the original while simultaneously revamping and updating the wraparound concept. Gone is the story of Billy. While he served as a sort of conduit through which viewers read ***Creepshow*** comics, viewers of the 2019 series get a POV look at each issue. During the stories, we are repeatedly brought back to the comic book panels, especially when transitioning from scene to scene. A variety of clever techniques are utilized to remind us that we're inside a comic book come to life. In this effort alone, this series proves itself worthy of the ***Creepshow*** legacy. Anthology filmmakers should look to it for ideas on how to make classic concepts feel fresh again.

• • •

CAT'S EYE (FILM, 1985)

1 DIRECTOR | RUNTIME: 1HR 34MIN

-Notable Cast/Crew: Writer Stephen King; Actors Drew Barrymore & James Woods

-Wraparound type: Thematic Throughline

-The setup: The shorts in this film are based on stories by Stephen King, and tied together by a stray cat. In New York City, the cat peers into a storefront window, drawn by a mannequin that comes to life as a girl, played by a young Drew Barrymore. The girl begs the cat to, "find it," but before he's able to learn more, he's swept up by a man and brought into a nearby building. It's here that we segue to our first short.

-First short: A different man enters the same building we just saw the cat taken into. He visits a clinic whose experimental methods will help him quit smoking, or so he hopes. When their methods progressively include stalking, electrocution, and torture, he regrets ever going to them.

-Return to wraparound: We return to the cat's story as it escapes captivity. But as this happens, the filmmakers crosscut to the first story to see how things end for its characters. This technique of returning to the wraparound while simultaneously concluding the first short helps the film maintain a sense of forward momentum.

As the cat roams around Atlantic City, he passes by an electronics store window, and this time sees Barrymore's character in a TV commercial. The girl again addresses the cat directly, beckoning him to, "find it." At this point, the cat crosses paths with the subjects of the next story.

-Second short: A dangerous mobster offers his wife's lover a sinister wager. The mobster proposes that if the lover can navigate the perimeter of a highrise apartment on a five inch ledge he'll let the lover and the wife go. While in the first short, the cat was present only for short bits of the story, much of this story is actually shown from the cat's perspective. And although I've made my best attempt to not make this a book of reviews, this is a fantastic short.

-Return to wraparound: After this short's ironic conclusion, the cat continues on his way, and finally arrives at the nice suburban home of none other than the girl from the store windows. They form a quick bond. When a mischievous troll comes out of the girl's bedroom wall every night, trying to kill her by stealing her breath, it will become the cat's responsibility to protect her.

-The takeaway: This is a movie that almost feels like it didn't need to be an anthology. While in most anthologies, the combined runtime of the wraparound segments is far less than the combined runtime of the shorts, the opposite is true in this movie. If you plan on making an anthology with a similar structure, you'd better make sure your shorts don't feel perfunctory. Fortunately, ***Cat's Eye*** dodged that bullet.

• • •

NIGHT TRAIN TO TERROR (FILM, 1985)

5 DIRECTORS | RUNTIME: 1HR 38MIN

-Wraparound type: Film Within a Film, Mind's Eye

-The setup: This film opens with a dance party on a train. A pop band struts their stuff while groupies dance like there's no tomorrow. The frame story, however, really gets going in an adjacent train car, where God and Satan sit at a table opposite from one another. The former is bathed in ethereal light while the latter is uplit ominously. They debate the values of righteousness and wickedness, and mention three people on the train who are destined to die. They look through the train window, their cosmic screen, and watch the story of their first subject.

-First short: A slasher uses a sanitarium as his torture chamber. Abducted young women are dismembered there; their body parts then sold to medical schools for research purposes. But when one of the several abductors working for the slasher has a change of heart, will he succeed in freeing those whom he's kidnapped?

-Return to wraparound: God and Satan debate over whether this abductor redeemed himself, and whether he deserves heaven or hell, eventually compromising on sending him to purgatory. Then their conversation moves to the nearby musicians as we're blessed with another music segment. Afterwards, God and Satan look through their cosmic screen as they judge "The Case of Gretta Connors,"

-Second short: This story involves a morbid secret society in which two members compete for the titular Gretta's hand.

-Return to wraparound: After watching her story, God insists he take Gretta to heaven, and Satan concedes. Despite this defeat, however, Satan insists his takeover of the Earth is coming to fruition as more and more humans are following his lead. With this, we transition to the band, where one of the groupies says how glad she is that the bus broke down and they had to take this train instead. The train's usher tells the groupies they're riding "the heaven express," while others call it "Satan's cannonball." The usher guarantees that, either way, this train delivers every passenger to their, "right destination."

-Third short: In "The Case of Claire Hansen," a detective investigates an immortal Nazi, but as he seeks to punish the Nazi for his war crimes, a much broader struggle between good and evil escalates.

-Return to wraparound: God and Satan argue over Claire's fate. Meanwhile the band keeps singing and the groupies keep dancing. In the end, the train crashes, as had been foreshadowed throughout the film, and God and the

Devil continue to argue over what will become of the many souls that have passed.

-The takeaway: When making a frame story that revolves around short films that have already been produced, as is the case with ***Night Train to Terror***, it's a convenient and clever plot device to have two characters debating the morality of the characters in said shorts. While it was a great creative choice to use God and the Devil as the characters in the frame story, the music video segments haven't aged well, and feel like filler. It'd be great to see this approached again with more modern sensibilities. In fact, for ***Gravedigger Dave Meets His Match***, I take a similar approach by soliciting shorts from other filmmakers and having my main characters discuss those shorts in the wraparound.

DEADTIME STORIES (1986)

1 DIRECTOR | RUNTIME: 1HR 33MIN

-Notable Cast/Crew: Director Jeffrey Delman; Editor William Szarka

-Wraparound type: Storytelling

-The setup: This anthology features reimaginings of three fables, but with a very 1980s sensibility. We start with a POV shot of a slasher making his way through a house, slowly moving towards the sound of a bed creaking rhythmically. We all know where this is heading… except we don't. The noise turns out to be a kid jumping on the bed and the POV isn't from a slasher at all, but the kid's uncle. He's babysitting for the night and agrees to tell his nephew a story to calm him down. With that, the frame story freezes and becomes a book cover. A hand reaches in and turns each page, revealing the film's credits.

-First short: The uncle tells the kid a loose adaptation of "Hansel and Gretel" in which two witches force their slave to assist them with increasingly cruel acts, all with the promise of eventual freedom.

-Return to wraparound: When the uncle is finished, the kid complains that the story had too happy of an ending, so the uncle revises it to end with a bit more blood.

-Second short: When the kid still can't sleep, he has the uncle tell him another story, this one an erotic werewolf drug-addled version of "Little Red Riding Hood." Yes, it's as strange as it sounds.

-Return to wraparound: The way this film crosscuts between the shorts and the uncle telling the stories feels similar to ***The Princess Bride***, which came out in 1987, the year after ***Deadtime Stories***.

-Third short: In this slapstick comedy version of "Goldilocks and the Three Bears," the titular heroine is a serial killer squatting in a house full of rotting corpses and the three bears are a family of mass murderers.

-Return to wraparound: When the uncle finishes this story, he leaves the kid to go to sleep, but it turns out there was a monster in his closet the whole time, ending the film with some 80s horror comedy goodness.

• • •

FROM A WHISPER TO A SCREAM AKA, THE OFFSPRING (FILM, 1987)

1 DIRECTOR | RUNTIME: 1HR 36MIN

-Notable Cast/Crew: Actor Vincent Price

-Wraparound type: Storytelling

-The setup: This film begins with the execution of a woman, witnessed by a small group of reporters and prison guards. Afterwards, one of the reporters travels to a historic library where she questions the woman's uncle about his involvement in her life of depravity. Through their dialogue, we learn that the now-dead woman began murdering as a child. But instead of admitting to having played a role in any of this, Vincent Price insists that they focus on their hometown of Oldfield itself, which he believes has been built on a foundation of suffering. Over the course of the movie he'll present the reporter with several documents and tell four stories which he hopes will illustrate his point.

-First short: We see a budding serial killer in the early stages of his murder spree. But how well will he fare when his victims start coming back to life?

-Return to wraparound: One interesting thing about this film is that each short takes place in an earlier time period than the previous. With each story, Price reaches further back into history to further prove his point; that the town itself is pure evil, not the people living in it.

-Second short: A hermit finds a shooting victim and saves his life by bestowing the gift of immortality upon him. But will the hermit end up regretting his choice?

-Return to wraparound: Price reaches even further back into history to prove his point.

-Third short: A glass-eater at a carnival falls in love with a townie, but not without certain consequences.

-Return to wraparound: Price shows the reporter a collection of town records as we transition to the final story.

Fourth short: As the Civil War comes to an end, the orphaned children of Oldfield take their revenge on the soldiers who continue to ravage the land.

-Return to wraparound: The film ends with a twist, as the reporter turns out to not be a reporter at all, but something much different.

-The takeaway: It's long been speculated that the band, The Offspring, got their name from this film, which at one time was released under the title, ***The Offspring***. As they're one of my all-time favorite bands, I tried reaching out to them in hopes they could give me more details about the film's influence. But alas, no reply.

A quick comparison of font choices between the film's poster and the band's early releases at least hints at the connection. The band's self-titled LP and their EP, ***Baghdad***, feature hand-drawn text that bears distinct resemblance to the aforementioned poster. In addition, a subsequent bootleg EP, ***They Were Born to Kill***, features the exact typography as the film, and the album's cover art depicts the opening execution scene from the film. The phrase "They were born to kill," is also found on the back cover of the movie's VHS release.

So what is the significance of all of this to a filmmaker? The band, who at the time were total unknowns, reappropriated the branding of the film for the branding of their band. While they were still trying to carve out their identity, the movie had legendary Vincent Price in it. Co-opting such star power would help them carve out an identity, but over time the band would actually become more well-known than the film. The anthology, ***Black Sabbath***, very similarly influenced the band of the same name.

So, my very long-winded takeaway is this: Always be cognizant of how your film may fit into the ever-growing pop-culture landscape. Perhaps there's a piece of pop-culture to which you'd like to link your film. I am reminded of the band, A Wilhelm Scream. Their name was co-opted from a popular production trope used in the ***Star Wars*** franchise and countless other films. To what degree does the band benefit from people searching for the production trope and finding the band entirely by accident? It was a similar series of events that first made me aware of ***From a Whisper to a Scream*** when I began researching my favorite band way back in 1994, so you never know.

1990s

TALES FROM THE CRYPT (SERIES, 1989-1996)

93 EPISODES | EPISODE RUNTIME: ~ 25MIN

-Notable Cast/Crew: Voice actor John Kassir

-Wraparound type: Horror Host

-The setup: Each episode begins with the Cryptkeeper, masterfully voiced by John Kassir, giving an introduction to the main story. His beady little eyes look right at us as he delivers clever puns and morbid jokes to prep us for each story. In later seasons, these intros became increasingly campy, but the Crypterkeeper never lost his charm. In the documentary, ***Tales from the Crypt: From Comic Books to Television***, Jack Wohl (President of Tales from the Crypt Productions) says, “The key to the Cryptkeeper is that he’s comedy relief. He sometimes can get a little ghoulish, but never really over the top. He’s there to ease the pain of being scared, perhaps.”

-A typical episode: The episode that actually interested me most for this book was the first episode of the first season, “The Man Who Was Death.” As I have an unending interest in layered storytelling, this episode is unique in that the fourth wall is broken on two levels. The first level, of course, is the Cryptkeeper, who introduces the story of a down-and-out executioner who moonlights as a vigilante.

One of the things that makes this episode so much fun is how the executioner repeatedly breaks the fourth wall as well. I can't say this for sure, as I haven't seen every single episode, but I doubt the Crypterkeeper allows many of his characters this level of freedom. He keeps most of them on a pretty tight leash, and usually leaves the audience for him to address, and him alone. It seems to me that the producers were still finding their preferred tone for the series, but in that process of discovery they released an incredibly fun first episode.

-The takeaway: Although this series is an adaptation of the EC comic book series of the same name, its host actually seems to be more influenced by the later Warren Publishing comic series, ***Creepy***. In fact, both ***Creepshow*** and HBO's ***Tales from the Crypt*** franchise seem to have taken particular inspiration from ***Creepy***'s host, Uncle Creepy. Both in appearance and attitude, from the 4th wall breaks to the way in which readers are addressed, the influence is clear. Like the version of the Cryptkeeper seen in the cartoon, ***Tales from the Cryptkeeper***, Uncle Creepy is prone to referring to readers as "kiddies" or "pain pals, " and makes reference to his, "deadtime stories."

This animated television series continues the horror-host approach from ***Tales from the Crypt***, featuring the Cryptkeeper as host, but with a decidedly kid-friendly approach. The open features a frightened boy making his way through the Cryptkeeper's mansion, until he's joined by a group of classic monsters, with whom he sits to enjoy a story from the show's skeletal host. In a typical episode, the Cryptkeeper will navigate via a monologue (full of cheesy horror puns) towards the main story. Addressing the camera, he'll open a dusty old book and segue to a horror comedy story that's usually, in all honesty, pretty good. While the Cryptkeeper interacts with the viewing audience in the bookend pieces, he'll sometimes also interact with the storylines or characters of the episode's featured segment. This allows for a metanarrative in which the Cryptkeeper acknowledges that he's in a TV show.

The franchise didn't stop at the animated series. It also spawned several feature films and even a game show for kids. The success of the franchise should, in my opinion, be attributed to the charisma of the Cryptkeeper himself. Filmmakers should always consider how their characters could help build a valuable intellectual property. I certainly am thinking along those lines with my character, Gravedigger Dave. I've always viewed him as a mashup between the Cryptkeeper and Ernest P. Worrell. Here's hoping that he's even half as successful as those two characters.

TWO EVIL EYES (FILM, 1990)

2 DIRECTORS | RUNTIME: 2HRS

-Notable Cast/Crew: Directors George A. Romero & Dario Argento; Actors Adrienne Barbeau & Harvey Keitel

-Wraparound type: Package film

-The setup: This Edgar Allan Poe adaptation begins with shots of real monuments to the famous horror author and a voiceover, which states that his stories inspired the movie. First up is the George A. Romero-directed adaptation of "The Facts in the Case of M. Valdemar."

-First short: This adaptation updates the source material to take place in the 90s. In this version, Valdemar has been put in a postmortem trace that keeps him in an undead state. Meanwhile, the people closest to him seek to steal his riches, until he morphs into a zombie and turns on them.

-Second short: Based on Poe's story, "The Black Cat," a man murders his live-in girlfriend and hides her corpse within the basement walls of his house. But has he made a fateful error that will lead to the discovery of his crime?

-The takeaway: At about an hour each, it's hard to call these films short. If you've made a long short, say 45 minutes or more, you've probably found that it has struggled making its way into festivals. It's too long to be a short, but too short to be a feature. I actually faced this dilemma when taking submissions for my anthology sequel, ***Gravedigger Dave Meets His Match***. I saw some great films that were 45+ minutes, but couldn't figure out how to include them in a film that I wanted to be fast paced.

If you are, however, a filmmaker with a 45+ minute short, what you could do is find another filmmaker who has a thematically similar 45+ minute film and package them together as a double-feature, like ***Two Evil Eyes***, or 2007's ***Grindhouse***.

• • •

TALES FROM THE DARKSIDE: THE MOVIE (FILM, 1990)

1 DIRECTOR | RUNTIME: 1HR 44MIN

-Notable Cast/Crew: Director John Harrison; Writer George A. Romero; Actors Debbie Harry, Julianne Moore, & Steve Buscemi

-Wraparound type: Storytelling

-Background: This film is loosely based on a TV series of the same name created by horror icon George A. Romero. In the season one DVD commentary he says, "It was sort of the hallmark of the ***Darkside*** series that we're actually looking at the flipside of the world where it's not a happy ending. In fact, it's very likely to be an unhappy ending."

Other than the notion of the "flipside" that Romero describes, there's nothing else that connects each episode. The movie takes the wraparound concept in a much different direction, weaving a narrative around a storyteller in a desperate situation.

-The setup: This anthology begins with a seemingly sweet woman driving home from the store. Along the way, she passes a pastor who reminds her not to miss choir. But inside her lovely home, she has locked a kid in a dungeon who she plans to cook for a dinner party later that evening. She tells him how she plans to disembowel and stuff him, not showing any hint of cruelty as she does so. It's all matter of fact for her, as if she's a school teacher explaining an upcoming exam to her student. In a moment of ingenuity, the kid offers to tell her a story to distract her. She has, afterall, given him her childhood books to read while in captivity.

-First short: Based on an Arthur Conan Doyle story, this short centers around a history student who summons a mummy to enact revenge on those who've wronged him.

-Return to wraparound: The filmmakers transition back to the wraparound by showing a set of sharp tools that seem to be in the short, but are then revealed to instead be a part of the frame story. It's a good piece of editing that helps transition between scenes, often called a "match cut." In the kitchen, the witch is sharpening her tools and warming the oven, making the kid increasingly nervous. But he is still able to convince her to listen to another story.

-Second short: An old man hires a hitman to kill a cat that has apparently slain several people. Definitely watch this short if you've been wanting to see a cat kill a man in the most gruesome way possible. This short could've fit perfectly into the 1977 anthology, ***The Uncanny***, which is all about killer cats.

-Return to wraparound: The kid convinces the witch to hear another story.

-Third short: A stone gargoyle outside an artist's studio comes to life, slaughters his friend, and tells him that he's never to speak of these events as long as he lives. When the man agrees, he's free to go. Minutes later, he meets a woman with whom he eventually has two children. But as the secret of the gargoyle gnaws at him, we begin to suspect that she's keeping a secret of her own from that night. This story is an update of one found in the 1964 Japanese anthology, ***Kwaidan***.

-Return to wraparound: The witch refuses to let the boy tell another story, but he goes into one anyway; his own. He narrates the events that led up to his abduction, followed by his plan to escape. Will he succeed? Watch and find out.

-The takeaway: You've probably noticed that I'm partial to anthologies in which the respective narratives of the wraparound and the shorts drive each other forward and are even intrinsic to one another. In the case of ***Tales from the Darkside***, the survival of our protagonist in the frame story is dependent on the quality of the shorts. As a result, the kid's plight is never far from our minds. We're hoping that these stories prove to be his means to escape. What's he plotting? Is he simply stalling? Such questions are the ingredients (no pun intended) for a tense frame story. Interweaving the character drama of the wraparound with the shorts is, for my money, the most effective way to approach an anthology.

• • •

THE SIMPSONS: TREEHOUSE OF HORROR (TV SPECIALS, 1990-CURRENT)

30 EPISODES | EPISODE RUNTIME: ~22MIN

-Notable Cast/Crew: Producer Al Jean

-Wraparound types: Storytelling, Mind's Eye, Tangential Throughline, Thematic Throughline, Package Film

-The setup: It should be noted that wraparound types differ greatly from episode to episode. The first **"Treehouse of Horror"** (ToH) special aired during the second season of the show. The shorts are tied together by stories Bart and Lisa are telling to each other in their backyard treehouse. In ToH II, Homer, Lisa and Bart binge on halloween candy as Marge warns them that if they don't ease up they'll get nightmares, which they unanimously laugh off. Of course, their nightmares make up the content of each short.

ToH III begins with a parody of ***Alfred Hitchcock Presents***. In the frame story of this episode, the Simpsons are throwing a Halloween party for the local kids, during which they each take turns telling scary stories. ToH V begins with Bart and Homer riffing on the classic ***Outer Limits*** open. This episode, however, does not have a wraparound story. In such episodes, Al Jean told me, “We initially had a framing narrative but as the shows got shorter it seemed like we could get more bang for our buck by having a funny cold open.”

-A typical episode: ToH specials often feature shorts that are based on a classic short story or a famous horror film. In one episode, they adapt the W.W. Jacobs’ short story, “The Monkey’s Paw,” in which the titular paw grants the Simpson family five wishes, but at a terrible cost. Another features a ***Frankenstein*** parody in which Mr. Burns removes Homer’s brain and transplants it into a robot’s body.

Sometimes the shorts are very loose adaptations. In ToH III, Bart (dressed as Alex from ***A Clockwork Orange***) tells a tale of zombie mayhem in Springfield. While this segment certainly draws from George A. Romero’s films in general, it doesn’t spoof any single film in particular.

One of my favorite ***Simpsons*** horror parodies is a spoof on ***A Nightmare on Elm Street*** in which Groundskeeper Willie haunts the dreams of Springfield’s kids. Another of my favorites, from ToH V, is a parody of ***The Shining***, which features the classic line, “No TV and no beer make Homer go crazy.”

-The takeaway: The folks behind ***The Simpsons*** created a series of specials that would serve as an entry-point to the would of horror for their younger viewers. Though I didn’t know it at the time, ***The Simpsons*** introduced me to classics like ***The Twilight Zone***, ***Alfred Hitchcock Presents***, ***The Shining***, ***A Nightmare on Elm Street***, ***The***

Outer Limits, ***Night Gallery***, and the W.W. Jacobs' classic short story "The Monkey's Paw."

I've wondered if it ever occurs to those in the writers' room that these episodes can serve as an early education in the genre. When I asked producer Al Jean, he replied, "We never hold back on obscure references and we feel that just as Mad Magazine introduced us to adult movies as a kid the "Treehouse" specials might serve as a child's introduction to Cthulu." To a very large degree, my horror fandom started with ***The Simpsons***.

The takeaway here is not to dismiss horror parody or horror comedy as irrelevant, even if it's your plan to take the genre seriously. Inspiration comes in many forms. Sometimes, genre parody can even be the purest expression of genre mastery.

Take, for instance, the ***Scared Shrekless*** Halloween TV special. In the frame story, the main characters travel to a creepy old castle where they try to scare each other away by telling stories next to a fireplace. This Storytelling anthology parodies ***Frankenstein***, ***Psycho*** and ***The Exorcist*** in a style not unlike "Treehouse of Horror." ***Scared Shrekless*** took me by surprise. It's really funny, and the parodies are truly clever. Like ***The Simpsons***, this special likely gave kids of a certain generation their first exposure to an essential group of horror tropes, and for that I applaud it. Again, inspiration comes in many forms.

ARE YOU AFRAID OF THE DARK? (SERIES, 1992-2000)

91 EPISODES | EPISODE RUNTIME: ~22MIN

-Notable Cast/Crew: Creator D.J. MacHale; Director Ron Oliver

-Wraparound type: Storytelling

-The setup: "Submitted for the approval of the Midnight Society..." If you're a child of the 90s and this line doesn't jazz you up, I'm not sure what will. The Midnight Society is made up of a group of kids who meet at a campfire to tell each other scary stories. Each kid takes a turn telling a story, and each story is the focus of a single episode.

-A typical episode: The main story of each episode often begins with a few lines of narration from that episode's storyteller to help transition from the campfire setting to the setting of the episode. The stories always center around kids, and they're always about the paranormal.

AYAOTD? Features a mix of original stories and adaptations of classic stories. Some particularly good episodes adapt, "The Monkey's Paw" and "The Headless Horseman," both of which were also parodied in ***The Simpsons***. The series' original scripts likewise feature things like haunted film reels, haunted comic books, and haunted cameras. Horror shows made for kids often get a bad rap, but children of the 90s are likely to remember ***AYAOTD?*** as pure horror gold. Rewatching it as an adult does not disappoint.

-The takeaway: As director Ron Oliver and I discussed in our Section I interview, this was a formative anthology for me. Not long after our interview, the first ***AYAOTD?*** episode in 19 years was released. I wasted no time giving it a watch. The 2019 reboot is interesting in that it provides a bit of an origin story for the Midnight Society. The first episode, "Submitted for Approval," centers around a new girl at school. She's given 24 hours to come up with a scary story to present to the legendary storytelling club. If the story is deemed scary enough, she'll be allowed to join as a permanent member.

It's an innovative approach to an anthology series. This new frame story deconstructs the original series in a creative way, and establishes the new season as a fresh take on the franchise. Like the season one finale of the 2019 ***Twilight Zone*** reboot, this show reimagines the original framing narrative by looking at it from the inside out. Challenge yourself to likewise deconstruct an established franchise. Perhaps you'll come up with something fresh that can serve as a jumping-off point for your own anthology.

BODY BAGS (FILM, 1993)

2 DIRECTORS | RUNTIME: 1HR 31MIN

-Notable Cast/Crew: Directors John Carpenter & Tobe Hooper; Actors Mark Hammill, Twiggy, Robert Carradine, & Wes Craven

-Wraparound type: Horror Host

-The setup: The host of this anthology, a medical examiner, breaks the fourth wall and laments to the viewer about how bored he is with deaths by natural causes. Violent deaths are what make his day. The first corpse that he decides to tell us about was found on a lonely stretch of highway. From here, we transition to the first short.

-First short: A woman spends her first shift working at a gas station trying to evade a serial killer. Directed by John Carpenter, this short has him revisiting many of the slasher tropes he helped establish in his masterpiece, ***Halloween***. He employs these tropes with the skill of a horror veteran, and yet this short film seems to be typically overlooked in critical assessments of his filmography. For fans of Carpenter, this short is not to be missed.

-Return to wraparound: Our host sifts through his collection of corpses, showing us a couple who've both been beheaded. He also finds a plastic bag full of red goop, telling us it's all that's left of a person who was dragged by a train as we transition to another segment directed by Carpenter.

-Second short: A balding man longs so deeply for a full head of hair that he'll volunteer for a questionable procedure, which inevitably backfires. Voluntary medical experiments gone awry serve as the jumping off point for many a horror short. 2013's ***Chilling Visions: 5 Senses of Fear*** would later revisit the concept of a procedure backfiring in a manner that is truly disgusting

-Return to wraparound: The medical examiner removes an eyeball from a jar, which brings us to the final segment.

-Third short: Mark Hamill gives a standout performance about a baseball player who loses an eye in a car accident. But when he volunteers for an experimental eye transplant, he'll begin to feel the influence of the eye's previous owner, who apparently was quite a violent fellow.

-Return to wraparound: Here, our host reveals the anthology's twist. It's a clever ending to a great movie.

-The takeaway: The most obvious thing to attribute this movie's awesomeness to is the talent involved. Though I doubt that if you're reading this book you have the ability to recruit John Carpenter and Tobe Hooper to direct the shorts in your anthology, there's still a ton of undiscovered directors out there who are eager to collaborate.

GOOSEBUMPS (SERIES, 1995-1998)

74 EPISODES | EPISODE RUNTIME: ~22 MIN

-Notable Cast/Crew: Writer R.L. Stine; Director Ron Oliver

-Wraparound type: Thematic Throughline, Horror Host

-The setup: In this show's opening sequence, a figure dressed in black approaches a village. His briefcase is engraved, "R.L. Stine," and is blown open by the wind. Pages upon pages come spilling out, infecting the town below with all manner of mischief and terror. Stine's manuscripts possess a supernatural quality, and their disbursement causes his stories to come to life. A similar approach would later be used in the 2015 ***Goosebumps*** film.

In some episodes this opening sequence is the only setup. In others, the show includes R.L. Stine himself as host. He gives a brief introduction to the episode's main story, oftentimes in a setting that relates to said story. For more on Stine's involvement in the series be sure to check out my interview with director Ron Oliver in Section 1.

-A typical episode: Episodes often begin with a fake scare. By this, I mean that something will frighten the main character just before the show dissolves to black for the first commercial break. Upon returning from the break, the scare is often revealed to be some sort of prank or a bit of trouble that the protagonist manages to get out of easily. This device has a dual function. The cliffhanger keeps viewers through the commercials, and the resolution of the scare reveals the traits of the character that will come back later when they're dealing with the real conflict of the episode. Likewise, the larger plot of the episode will sometimes turn out to be a false scare. I won't tell you which ones though. I wouldn't want to kill the suspense.

One of the best things about this series is there's a plethora of two-parters. This allowed for nearly unabridged adaptations of the original novels. Amongst my favorites is "One Day at Horrorland," which leads us through a theme park full of fun scares. But the second part launches into a fairly brilliant bit of genre deconstruction. This is a truly bizarre episode that's best described as ***The Monster Club*** meets ***Running Man***.

Another of my favorite episodes is "Be Careful What You Wish For." When an unpopular high school basketball player helps a witch, the witch grants the girl three wishes. Inevitably, the wishes backfire one by one. (I'm often drawn to stories about wishes gone wrong.)

-The takeaway: In 2018, filmmaker Matt Rasmussen (who also plays Gravedigger Dave) made the definitive documentary, ***Goosebumps - The Saga of Scares***. The doc shows the absolute mountain of content that's been released under the ***Goosebumps*** banner since 1992. The man himself, R.L. Stine, shared it several times social media, writing on Facebook, "Here's the most amazing video about ***Goosebumps*** ever made." Cover artist Tim Jacobus likewise wrote on Facebook, "Wow! Even I learned a couple of things!"

When I asked my good buddy Rasmussen his thoughts on the longevity of the franchise he had this to say:

> I think one of the reasons ***Goosebumps*** has endured is because it's bigger than a series of children's books. It's a multi-platformed franchise that is ripe for films, television, video games, etc. There are literally hundreds of stories involving numerous characters, including the iconic monsters. Kids can really latch into a particular character or idea that speaks to them. And each story is so rich and well-conceived, there's something to love about each and every story!

Matt highlights one of the most important things for filmmakers to take away from the ***Goosebumps*** TV series. The books are so full of engaging characters and storylines, they lend themselves to endless interpretation. Today, we're living in a much different world than the early 90s, when ***Goosebumps*** was first adapted. Independent filmmakers don't necessarily have to go to traditional publishers to find material to adapt. There are thousands of independent horror writers online, publishing through platforms like Kindle Unlimited, or getting their work printed in short story anthologies.

Find a story you like from an indie writer and look up their other publications. You might just stumble upon a body of work as engaging and ripe for adaptation as Stine's work was in the 90s. And chances are that this hypothetical indie author is hoping for their opportunity to get noticed. They might see an indie horror anthology film as a way to make that happen, and let you adapt their work for free.

My point, here, is that, when looking at a successful anthology TV series like ***Goosebumps***, don't beat yourself up if you think you'll never write as good as Stine. The vast majority of us never will. But somewhere out there is an undiscovered indie writer with a treasure trove of material. Find that person. Partner with them. Option their material. Make something great.

I know that's an oversimplification of what could be a very tedious process, but it's a manner of thinking that will dictate my next foray into horror anthologies. I'll be publishing a series of horror novellas under the banner, ***Gravedigger Dave Presents***. I have too many screenplays collecting dust that I can't afford to film. My hope is that, in prose-form, they'll be able to attract the attention of someone who can afford to produce them as films. It's a longshot, but you never know.

NECRONOMICON: BOOK OF THE DEAD (FILM, 1993)

RUNTIME: 1 HR 36 MIN | 3 DIRECTORS

-Wraparound type: Storytelling

-The setup: The anthology begins with a man giving a voiceover about how he learned that the notorious Book of the Dead is being hidden in America. We soon realize he's a fictionalized version of author H. P. Lovecraft. As he arrives at a sacred library we can tell it holds many secrets. Lovecraft steals a key and sleuths his way through the vaults until he comes upon this "Necronomicon." As he pages his way through the book, strange machinations begin all throughout the building. Gears turn as the demonic structure seems to come to life and the book's guards mobilize. As Lovecraft begins reading a story (and copying by hand as he does so) we transition to the first short.

-First short: When the heir to a wealthy estate comes to survey his inheritance, the executor of the estate takes him on a tour, giving him a review of the family's tragic history. We learn that our protagonist has traveled to the estate in hopes of locating the "Book of the Dead," which is confirmed to be on the grounds. But, like his ancestors, this man will come to regret his fateful attempts to wield its power.

-Return to wraparound: The guards are closing in as Lovecraft continues copying stories.

-Second short: This short features a story within a story; a flashback shows how an ordinary person fell in love with a walking corpse. Meanwhile, a reporter in present day is determined to learn the truth about the bizarre couple.

-Return to wraparound: The guards, and the building itself, are closing in on Lovecraft. He grows increasingly nervous for his safety as he begins the final story.

-Third short: Two officers pursue a suspect in a high-speed chase. After their cruiser flips, one of the injured officers is dragged away by the suspect. His partner draws her weapon and follows the trail of blood he leaves behind. She finds a bloody mess of gore and tentacles that is somewhat beyond description. I'd rather you watch it that read my attempt to put it into words.

-Return to wraparound: Lovecraft barely manages to escape the cursed library, but he does so with the book in hand. In the final moments of this anthology, as Lovecraft's car speeds away, we know that he's secured the source from which he'll derive his stories forever after.

-**The takeaway:** The Necronomicon featured in this film is a fictional book of spells that's appeared in several stories by renowned horror author H.P. Lovecraft. Like ***The Monster Club*** before it, this film constructs a metanarrative in which a fictionalized version of the author serves as the wraparound's protagonist. Thus, the shorts are presented as being the inspiration *for* the author's work rather than being inspired *by* the author's work.

While not anthology films themselves, the 2015 ***Goosebumps*** film and its 2018 sequel similarly deconstruct an author's work in meta fashion. The 2019 adaptation of the short story anthology, ***Scary Stories to Tell in the Dark*** would also take a similar approach, merging various anthology stories into a single narrative. Consider an author whose work you could possibly give a similar treatment. The approach is tried and true. Perhaps there are stories in the Public Domain that you could adapt without having to pay royalties. This is exactly the reason the works of both Lovecraft and Poe have been so widely adapted.

• • •

TALES FROM THE HOOD (FILM, 1995)

1 DIRECTOR | RUNTIME: 1HR 38MIN

TALES FROM THE HOOD 2 (FILM, 2018)

2 DIRECTORS | RUNTIME: 1HR 51MIN

-Notable Cast/Crew: Actor Clarence Williams III; Writers Rusty Cundieff & Darin Scott

-Wraparound type: Storytelling

-The setup: The first film begins with three drug dealers arriving at a funeral home. The mortician, a very bizarre and intense man, has been waiting for them. He apparently has found a large cache of drugs and plans to give it to them, but not before telling them the stories of some of the corpses he has lying around.

-First short: A rookie cop witnesses fellow officers murdering a black activist. The activist later appears in the rookie's vision, saying, "Bring them to me." So on the anniversary of the activist's death, the rookie leads the crooked cops to the activist's headstone, where his corpse can have its revenge on all of them.

-Return to wraparound: The mortician leads the dealers through the funeral home towards "the shit," but not before telling the story of another corpse.

-Second short: When a boy is being terrorized by a monster in his home, his teacher vows to get to the bottom of it. Like the first short, this one is a story of revenge in which a victim gets to enact terrible vengeance over his tormentors.

-Return to wraparound: The mortician says a doll he keeps in the home is, "a way station for lost souls." His next story, which bears some stylistic similarity to ***Puppet Master***, tells the story of this doll.

-Third short: When a racist politician moves into a house that was the site of a brutal slave massacre, he learns that the souls of the murdered slaves were put into dolls. When the politician ignores all warnings, and opts to stay in the house, the doll makes him pay for his racist beliefs.

-Return to wraparound: The drug dealers are growing impatient, but that doesn't stop the mortician from telling another tale.

-Fourth short: When a trigger-happy murderer agrees to a behavior modification program in exchange for an early prison release, the treatment proves to be more akin to ***A***

Clockwork Orange than he expected. This is by far the craziest short in the anthology.

-Return to wraparound: The dealers were actually more involved in the events of the fourth short than they'd like to admit. Will the mortician let them off easy, or make them pay for their crimes?

-The sequel's setup: In the second film, released over two decades later, a storyteller is hired by a particularly racist and sexist AI developer. The storyteller must help the AI (an android cop) learn to choose between incarceration and execution on the spot. The filmmakers don't hold back in showing us what a bigot the AI developer is. Before transitioning to the first short, the storyteller breaks the fourth wall to address the audience, and promises the segment will draw parallels to the Black Lives Matter movement.

-**First short:** This segment re-imagines a trope often seen in anthologies; that of the possessed doll come to life. This interpretation of the trope, however, serves as an examination of modern day racism. Like the shorts in the first ***Tales from the Hood***, is a horror-themed commentary on the manifestations of racism in modern culture.

-Return to wraparound: As each short concludes, a psychedelic data-flow animation brings us back to the frame story, while a voiceover says, "The tale has been successfully stored in the Patriot's memory." The developer says he's looking for a story about crime. The storyteller promises he can deliver.

-Second short: Several gangsters have taken a man hostage, hoping he'll reveal the location of his riches. But in the process of beating the info out of him, they accidentally kill him. Their solution to this predicament is to force a phony TV psychic into channeling the murdered man's ghost, who will then give up the location of his riches. Needless to say, things go horribly and hilariously wrong for the gangsters.

-Return to wraparound: Again, the story is stored in the Patriot's memory, the developer acts like a moron, and the storyteller tells another story.

-Third short: Two guys drug their Tinder dates with plans to rape them, but things aren't as they seem when the two girls reveal their fangs.

-Return to wraparound: We basically see more of the same, but don't give up this anthology. There's something behind the storyteller's motivations in selecting these particular tales that won't be revealed until the end.

-Fourth short: A pregnant woman sees the ghost of a black boy who was tortured by two racist white men. But what connection does the past have to her baby, and what does the baby's father have to learn about racism in today's world?

-Return to wraparound: We learn the storyteller's true motivations. He's told his final story just in time for a press conference. The developer goes on a wildly racist rant before revealing the Patriot to the world. But the storyteller seems to know something nobody else does. Unbeknownst to the developer, the AI was listening not only to the storyteller's tales, but also the conversations in between tales. In front of the press, the developer instructs the Patriot to use excessive force in hunting criminals that pose a threat to America. When the AI turns on it's creator, what follows is the epitome of b-movie excellence.

-**The takeaway:** Socially conscious horror is a brand in short supply. That's only one aspect that makes ***Tales from the Hood***, and it's sequel, so unique. ***Tales from the Hood 2*** wasn't the only anthology of this ilk released by Rusty Cundieff and Darin Scott in 2018. They also released ***American Nightmares*** starring Danny Trejo. I suspect that the extended development of ***Tales from the Hood 2*** left the filmmakers with a plethora of short film concepts that they didn't want to see go to waste. The shorts in ***American Nightmares*** do, after all, adhere to a similar brand of social commentary that fans of theirs have become accustomed to. I recommend both to any anthology filmmaker. Releasing two features in one year is a feat to be admired.

QUICKSILVER HIGHWAY (FILM, 1997)

1 DIRECTOR | RUNTIME: 1HR 30MIN

-Notable Cast/Crew: Actor Christopher Lloyd; Director Mick Garris; Writers Stephen King & Cliver Barker

-Wraparound type: Storytelling

-The setup: As the title suggests, this anthology begins on a lonely stretch of desert highway. When a pair of newlyweds get a flat, the groom hikes ahead in search of the nearest town. Meanwhile the bride, still in her wedding dress, stays behind with the car. As night falls, she becomes increasingly anxious, until she sees a pair of headlights in the dark. It's not her husband in the approaching rig, but a vagabond collector of stories going by the name of Quicksilver, and played by Christopher Lloyd. She cautiously accepts his invitation to join him in his trailer, which he's decorated to compete with the most immaculate of dining rooms. Here, he tells her one of the stories he's collected on his travels, which he promises will reveal to her the truth of America's ugly underbelly.

-First short: A father (played by the same actor as the groom) struggles through a dust storm, trying to drive home in time for his son's birthday. After stopping for gas, he purchases a set of windup teeth for his son, and agrees to pick up a hitchhiker who he passed on the side of the road earlier. But when the hitchhiker reveals his true intentions, the teeth will come to life in defense of their new owner.

-Return to wraparound: The bride asks if there was a moral to the story. Quicksilver replies, "Must every story have a moral point?" After a moment of debate on this subject, the two characters hear a crash outside. Out of the wreck, the chattering teeth make a dramatic reappearance.

At this point, ***Quicksilver Highway*** concludes the bride's story and introduces a second wraparound at a carnival. Here, we follow a pickpocket as he steals with near-supernatural ease. When an observant woman calls out for the police, he slinks away to hide inside an exhibit that promises stories of horror. It is, of course, Quicksilver's trailer, redecorated as a museum for the occasion. Inside, Quicksilver goes on about a person's hands, and what they might be without them. The story seems especially relevant to the thief, as we transition to the next short.

-Second short: The hands of a plastic surgeon (played by the same actor who portrays the thief) rebel against him, leading to a hospital-wide revolution of severed hands against their bodies in a horror-comedy short that's reminiscent of ***Evil Dead II*** and ***Addams Family***.

-Return to wraparound: When we return to the frame story, Quicksilver again insists that his stories have no moral. But as the pickpocket leaves the exhibit, and his hands begin to defy him, he will soon learn the consequences of his thievery.

-The takeaway: Similar to ***Unheimliche Geschichten***, this anthology adds a layer of thematic connection by having the actors in the frame story play different characters in the short segments. In ***Quicksilver Highway***, this has the effect of allowing us to see each story from the perspective of the listener, as they imagine themselves and their loved ones experiencing the events of which Quicksilver speaks.

Perhaps this makes it more troubling for the bride when Quicksilver asks her, “Must every story have a moral point?” In this moment, he seems to speak for many horror anthologies, in which things seem to just happen. There are no three acts, no hero’s journey, no lesson learned. As the bride sees for herself, sometimes things just happen.

2000s

TERROR TRACT (FILM, 2000)

2 DIRECTORS | RUNTIME: 1HR 36MIN

-Notable Cast/Crew: Actors Scott Ritter & Bryan Cranston

-Wraparound type: Storytelling

-The setup: Scott Ritter stars in this film's wraparound as a real estate agent driving two newlyweds around a neighborhood to look at houses. In the first house, he ominously tells them that he's obligated to disclose the house's history and begins telling them a story.

-First short: A husband leaves on business as his wife welcomes her lover into their home for the night. When the husband sneaks back home, fully expecting to find the two together, he goes off the deep end, trying to kill them both in a most sadistic way. How will the victors of this fight to the death be able to cope with the consequences of their actions?

-Return to wraparound: This short transitions back to the frame story in a very creative way, as Ritter's character steps into the final frame of the short and the characters from the short fade away. The technique creates a seamlessness that makes the segue back to the wraparound feel organic. Before you make your anthology, watch this transition. In all of the anthology films I've watched it's one of the smoothest I can recall.

When the couple opts out of this house, the realtor's emotions get the better of him and he reveals a bit of desperation. He says a sale today would solidify a bonus he's been after, but can we trust him? Subtleties in his performance lead the audience to infer he has an ulterior motive that's yet to be revealed, adding tension to the frame story. At the next house, the realtor cautions against pets as he tells the story of the previous occupants.

-Second short: Bryan Cranston plays a father whose daughter brings home a stray monkey she finds in the backyard. When the daughter and mother fall in love with the new family pet, Cranston seems to be the only one who sees the monkey's evil side. The monkey, in turn, starts to bring out Cranston's evil side in this over-the-top comedy/thriller.

-Return to wraparound: Having heard the story of this second house, the couple rushes out. When Ritter gets a call from a man we presume is his boss, he seems unreasonably nervous. Ritter is able to convince the couple to see a third, and when the wife insists on knowing the history of the house, Ritter nervously tells them.

-Third short: A teen visits a psychiatrist unannounced and tells her he's had telepathic visions of her death at the hands of a notorious serial killer.

Return to wraparound: This is enough to make the couple want to cut and run. It's here that Ritter's secret, and the true nature of this neighborhood, are finally revealed. The end of this anthology is beautiful, brutal, and hilarious, with Ritter showing he knows how to play a character going off the deep end. The finale is horror comedy perfection.

-The takeaway: The plot device of the realtor telling stories to prospective homebuyers would later be used in the second ***Volumes of Blood*** film. Viewing these two films back-to-back showed me that it's okay to use plot devices that have been used before, so long as you're able to put your own spin on it.

THREE (FILM, 2002)

(RELEASED IN THE U.S. AS 3... EXTREMES II)

3 DIRECTORS | RUNTIME: 2HR 20MIN

THREE... EXTREMES (FILM, 2004)

3 DIRECTORS | RUNTIME: 2HR 5 MIN

-Notable Cast/Crew: Directors Fruit Chan, Park Chan-wook, & Takashi Miike

-Wraparound type: Package Film

-The setup: Are you ready to be confused? Because when you look this film series up you're bound to be confused, unless I'm able to clear things up. Here goes. The first film in this series, ***Three***, was released in 2002, but not in America. In 2004, a sequel was made called ***Three… Extremes***, and was released in America. Because of the sequel's popularity, the first film, ***Three***, was finally released in America, but not as ***Three***. It was released as ***3… Extremes II***. So, if you're in America and you watch ***3... Extremes II***, you are actually watching the first film. If you watch ***Three… Extremes***, you are actually watching the second film. It took me a little while to wrap my head around this.

While the first film in this franchise is certainly worth your time, the sequel is something of a masterpiece and will be my focus here. This Package Film launches right into the first short without any sort of framing device.

-First short: Directed by Fruit Chan, a seemingly kind and youthful cook charges an exorbitant price for her homemade dumplings made of ground baby meat, promising them to be the secret to eternal youth. Yup, baby meat. It's actually handled in a dryly funny manner believe it or not. When the cook's latest client learns what is really in these precious dumplings, will her guilt and disgust outweigh her vanity? Or will she actually begin to enjoy this upper-class brand of cannibalism?

-Second short: As the title of the anthology series suggests, it only gets more extreme from here. Of all the horror anthologies I've watched (and I've watched quite a few), this anthology's second short, "Cut," is one of the more gripping films I've ever seen. Directed by Park Chan-wook, perhaps most famous for ***Oldboy***, this film begins with an exquisitely executed long take; the sort that fully immerses the viewer in the physical environment of the story. And this shot is only the first of the filmmaker's clever technical executions. In this short, an actor takes revenge against a filmmaker for what he sees as a disregard for his talent. The manner of the revenge is so bizarre it'd be futile to describe it here. Be sure to watch this short. To call it intense is an understatement.

-Third short: In this final segment, directed by the controversial Takashi Miike, a writer has recurring nightmares about her own murder and believes her publisher to be her attacker. But could the guilt of something she did as a child be the cause of these dreams? And will her premonition come to pass? Of the three films in the anthology, this is the most contemplative and introspective, but that's not to say that it's any less disturbing than the others.

-The takeaway: This film series is an interesting example of how you might thematically link horror segments that don't, at least at surface level, have anything to do with each other. In the marketing of the film, audiences learned that each of the three segments was made by a director from a different Asian country. Within the film, though, there's little that would indicate that fact. Each segment is in a different language, but that wouldn't be apparent to most English-speaking viewers. So, these are package films in the truest sense. Each short begins and ends with nothing joining it to the previous or the next. That's not to say that they aren't outstanding anthologies.

TRAPPED ASHES (FILM, 2006)

5 DIRECTORS | RUNTIME: 1HR 45MIN

-Notable Cast/Crew: Director Joe Dante

-Wraparoundtype: Storytelling

-The setup: When a tour of a Hollywood studio leads seven characters to a house that has been deemed off limits, they find that all passages lead to one room, and that they are unable to find an exit. It is at this point that, in a very self-aware fashion, the tour guide tells them all about the room's place in anthology movie history. He suggests that some unseen person has orchestrated their confinement, and that they're meant to reenact the plot of the fictional anthology, *Mysteria*. After a bit of arguing over what they should do, they agree to swap scary stories.

-First short: An actress who seeks surgery for breast enhancement rejects the standard procedures and instead agrees to participate in an experimental procedure that uses tissue from cadavers. Needless to say, things take a turn for the worse.

-Second short: In this anime-inspired animation/live action hybrid, a woman is sexually assaulted by an evil spirit while traveling with her husband in Japan.

-Third short: The third member of the tour tells a story about a filmmaker he once knew named Stanley. This fictionalized version of Stanley Kubrick and the story's narrator both fall in love with the same woman, and must slowly unravel the details of her demonic nature.

-The fourth short: Unlike the previous three, this short is narrated by the storyteller for the duration. She tells the strange story of her birth, and how she shared her mother's womb with a tapeworm, with which she forms a horrific bond.

-Return to wraparound: The tour guide reveals himself to be the orchestrator of their confinement, and reveals to each storyteller how their tale will end. There are brief scenes in which the loose ends from each short are tied up, allowing each character to come to the revelation that the events he speaks of are not premonitions, but have already happened. Like several of the Amicus anthologies that ***Trapped Ashes*** alludes to, these characters are already dead.

-The takeaway: Of course, *Mysteria* is not a real anthology film. But in ***Trapped Ashes*** it serves as a stand-in for the legendary Amicus films, like ***Vault of Horror*** and the original ***Tales from the Crypt***. In this way, ***Trapped Ashes*** is something of a love letter to the anthology films of that era, and for that reason it's certainly worth a watch.

GRINDHOUSE (FILM, 2007)

6 DIRECTORS | RUNTIME: 3HR 11MIN

-Notable Cast/Crew: Directors Quinten Tarantino, Robert Rodriguez, & too many talented folks to mention

-Wraparound type: Thematic Throughline, Package Film

-The setup: This anthology takes a pretty original approach in connecting each segment. While there is no overt wraparound, there is an interesting framing device built into the presentation of the anthology. This film asks audiences to imagine they are watching a movie in another time and another place. You're not in the comfort of your own home, you're in a filthy theater in the 1970s. Armed with this suspension of disbelief, the filmmakers present two main stories, with several faux movie trailers in between to serve as the connective tissue.

-First film: ***Grindhouse*** opens with 70s-style graphics not often seen today, and then goes right into the 105 minute-long ***Planet Terror*** segment, without ever acknowledging that the film is part of a larger anthology. In this film, a ragtag group of survivors must ward off the "sickos" that are tearing their town apart.

-Fake trailers: After ***Planet Terror***, we're shown five movie trailers (which are actually the best part of this anthology in my opinion): ***Machete***, ***Werewolf Women of the SS***, ***Don't***, ***Thanksgiving***, and ***Hobo with a Shotgun***. Though these were in fact fake trailers at the time of their production, they actually wound up leading to three spinoff feature films: ***Hobo with a Shotgun***, ***Machete***, and ***Machete Kills***.

-Second film: After the hilarious procession of fake trailers, we transition by way of 70s-style graphics to the next film in this double-feature: ***Death Proof***. In this film, Kurt Russel stalks a group of young women in an unstoppable muscle car. But these women prove to be more than Russel's character bargained for. The stunts are spectacular, and the finale is beyond intense.

-The takeaway: ***Grindhouse*** is perhaps the best example of how the shorts in an anthology can serve as a proof-of-concept for a spinoff feature film. While ***SiRen*** spun off from ***V/H/S***, and ***The Terrifier*** spun off from ***All Hallows' Eve***, three features spinning off from a single anthology, as with ***Grindhouse***, must be a record. The more I've noticed this the more I've considered how one of my ***Gravedigger Dave's Halfway House*** shorts might serve as a good proof-of-concept for a feature. Consider which of your short films, or short film concepts, might be ripe for a feature film treatment.

TRICK 'R TREAT (FILM, 2007)

1 DIRECTOR | RUNTIME: 1HR 22MIN

-Notable Cast/Crew: Director Michael Dougherty; Editor Michael Ivison; Actors Anna Paquin & Dylan Baker

-Wraparound type: Tangential Throughline

-The setup: In this immensely popular cult classic, characters are punished for disobeying the unwritten rules of Halloween. In the opening sequence, a woman is slaughtered for taking down decorations before Halloween night has ended. After her husband discovers her corpse hanging amongst the decorations, we cut to the comic book-style opening credits. The look harkens back to the first two ***Creepshow*** films. In this sequence we see covers for various comics starring the iconic character Sam, as well as panels depicting the segments to come.

Dylan Baker's character sums up the film's theme early in the second segment, saying, "My dad taught me tonight is about respecting the dead because this is the one night that the dead (and all sorts of other things) roam free and pay us a visit." He says this to a kid who has committed the mortal sin of taking all of the candy from a bowl marked, "take one." This kid will of course get what he has coming to him.

-The shorts: This anthology features several other narratives that interweave with one another. A shy girl played by Anna Paquin arrives in town with her friends, who're looking to party. While they seem harmless enough at first, there's something sinister behind their facade. All the while, ***Trick r' Treat***'s poster child Sam watches on.

Simultaneously, a group of costumed kids walk to an abandoned quarry on the outskirts of town as one girl tells the story of a school bus that crashed into it years ago. They plan to leave jack-o-lanterns as offerings for the students who died on the bus that day, but there's something else awaiting them in the foggy abyss. Sam bears witness to all of it, past and present.

The climactic scene starrs Brian Cox, and interweaves with Dyan Baker's segment and the quarry segment in unexpected ways. In this one, we get to see Sam in action, as he punishes an old man who takes glee in scaring off trick or treaters so he can steal their candy; an unforgivable Halloween sin.

Of course, my description of these shorts oversimplifies this amazing anthology to a great degree. The shorts don't play out one after another, but rather all unfold simultaneously, flowing into and out of each other with such subtlety that you might not even notice the transitions.

-Return to Wraparound: At the end of the anthology, all characters from all storylines converge. We see how the first pre-credit short connects to the larger story, and how all who break the rules of Halloween will get what they have coming to them. In a narrative sense, Sam exists to bear witness to the overlapping events of the anthology, and to enforce the film's code of ethics.

-The takeaway: The editing technique I describe above is not unlike the interwoven plot structures of films like ***Pulp Fiction***, ***Crash*** and ***Traffic***, or even romantic comedies like ***Love Actually***. ***Trick 'r Treat*** is a horror anthology whose plot structure is not necessarily informed by other horror anthologies. By totally eschewing the convention that one short must be completed before the next can begin, this film makes for a very different viewing experience than many of the others analyzed in this book. Breaking the mold has helped it stand apart and reach a level of popularity often uncommon amongst horror anthology films. I could go on about ***Trick 'r Treat***'s unique structure, but editor Robert Ivison breaks it down better than I ever could in our Section I interview.

2010s - 2020s

CHILLERAMA (FILM, 2011)

4 DIRECTORS | RUNTIME: 1HR 38MINS

-Notable Cast/Crew: Directors Adam Rifkin & Adam Green

-Wraparound type: Film Within a Film, Tangential Throughline

-The setup: The anthology begins with a man digging up his wife's grave to fulfill one last sexual fantasy. To his dismay, she awakens from the dead as a zombie and bites his balls off, beginning the process of his transformation into a zombie. Despite all this, he's a dedicated employee and must still get to work. His job just happens to be at a drive-in theater, and tonight just so happens to be the final installment of a long-running, wildly popular film fest: "Chillerama." Here, we meet festival goers and festival staffers with whom we'll watch each short film. And we'll return to these characters in between each short film to see how their evening progresses.

-First short: "Wadzilla," is a Godzilla spoof about a sperm that grows to epic size and rampages through a city.

-Second short: A homoerotic ***Grease*** parody entitled, "I was a teenage werebear."

-Third short: "The Diary of Anne Frankenstein," depicts Hitler making a monster out of body parts from his concentration camps. But the tables are quickly turned on the evil dictator, as the short becomes an over-the-top revenge fantasy.

-Return to wraparound: At this point in the anthology, it seems like we're about to watch a fourth short, as a bizarre mock-commercial for poop plays out. But it's actually a decoy, as the fourth story, "Zom-B-Movie," actually takes place within the frame story. Things take a turn for the worse at the drive-in, as the zombie plotline that began in the anthology's first scene devolves into an undead massacre.

But then, in very meta fashion, the film transitions to a final segment, which takes place in a very ordinary movie theater. Here, a group of horror fans who have been watching ***Chillerama*** with us begin to critique the anthology. These horror fans are actually ***Chillerama***'s four directors, and not all of them are happy with the movie they just watched.

-The takeaway: For another fun movie that features the director giving tongue-in-cheek commentary on his own movie, be sure to check out ***Volumes of Blood***.

BLACK MIRROR (SERIES, 2011-CURRENT)

22 EPISODES | EPISODE RUNTIME: VARIES FROM 40MIN TO 1HR+

-Notable Cast/Crew: Creator Charlie Brooker; Editor Stephen Haren

-Wraparound Type: Thematic Throughline, Storytelling

-The setup: In a 2011 article published by TheGuardian.com, series creator Charlie Brooker writes, "The 'black mirror' of the title is the one you'll find on every wall, on every desk, in the palm of every hand: the cold, shiny screen of a TV, a monitor, a smartphone."

For the first several seasons, this broad thematic concept was the show's only throughline. Each episode would begin with a cracked screen revealing the series title, and was apt to have a dependably depressing ending, but the connective tissue ended there. That is, until the episode, "Black Museum," hinted at a shared universe.

-A typical episode: The plot of "Black Museum" centers around a woman, Nish, who enters a museum to kill time. (At least, we're meant to think that she's there to kill time.) Displayed in the museum are several props from previous episodes, bringing new depth to the series as a whole. This, however, is not the primary reason the episode should be of interest to anthology filmmakers. "Black Museum" also features a storytelling structure quite similar to the Amicus anthologies of the 60s and 70s.

While at the museum, curator Rolo, tells Nish the backstory behind some of the exhibits, thus transitioning to several short films within the episode. So it's a Storytelling anthology within a Thematic Throughline anthology. Curious about how all of these elements were put into practice, I reached out to Stephen Haren, the editor of "Black Museum," to see what he could share about the episode's construction. Make sure you check out our conversation in Section I.

"Black Museum" was actually not the first ***Black Mirror*** episode that took this approach. The holiday special, "White Christmas" also utilized a storytelling anthology structure. The episode stars Jon Hamm and Rafe Spall, whose characters join each other in the kitchen of a decrepit bungalow that they have apparently both been stuck in for five years. We don't know why they're stuck there, but we do know that, despite their proximity, the two men have barely spoken. So, at Hamm's insistence, they sit down for a Christmas drink and swap stories.

Both of these episodes have extremely clever plot twists, and astonishingly smooth transitions and pacing. These episodes, like classic Amicus anthologies discussed earlier in Section II, create a sense of mystery surrounding the storytellers, hinting that the content of the short films will impact storytellers in some way.

-The takeaway: After writing about these two ***Black Mirror*** episodes I went back to see if there was another anthology series that released an anthology episode. As far as I can tell, ***Black Mirror*** is the first. This element alone makes the show worth your time. If that isn't enough, definitely watch it for its unique flavor of pessimistic futurism. This is one of the most captivating anthology series since the original ***Twilight Zone***.

• • •

V/H/S (FILM, 2012)

10 DIRECTORS | RUNTIME: 1 HR 56MIN

V/H/S 2 (FILM, 2013)

7 DIRECTORS | RUNTIME: 1HR 36MINS

V/H/S: VIRAL (FILM, 2014)

5 DIRECTORS | RUNTIME: 1HR 21MIN

-Notable Cast/Crew: Producer Brad Miska; Writer Simon Barrett; Director Roxanne Benjamin

-Wraparound type: Found Footage, Film Within a Film

-The setup: The first ***V/H/S*** movie opens with found footage of a group of guys reminiscent of Alex and his Droogs from ***A Clockwork Orange***. They videotape themselves molesting women, committing acts of vandalism, and talking about how they sell the footage online. They're hired for a mysterious job; to break into a house and retrieve a VHS tape. They find the house abandoned, except one room with a corpse in a chair and several staticky TV sets. There are tons of VHS tapes scattered about. One guy is left behind in this room while the others leave to explore the basement. Alone now, the guy puts a tape in the VCR.

-First short: Some bros hop between bars, hunting for girls, while one of them wears a pair of glasses with a cam/mic combo hidden inside. When they bring two girls back to their room, one of them reveals a black tongue and vampire teeth. She grows bat-like wings and takes revenge on the would-be rapist. (This short would later be expanded into a feature film, ***SiREN***.)

-Return to wraparound: In the basement, the guys find the tape that they're being paid to steal. Suddenly, a naked man scurries by and disappears in the shadows. Back in the room with the corpse, the guy left alone puts in another tape.

-Second short: A boyfriend and girlfriend get a knock on their motel room door from a strange girl looking for a ride. That night, an intruder enters their room, watches them sleep, and takes some money. The next night, the intruder arrives again, this time with more malicious intentions. How are all of these overnight incidents connected? Does the girlfriend know more than she's letting on?

-Return to wraparound: The corpse has disappeared, but the guy watching the tapes hasn't noticed.

-Third short: A group of college kids, two gals and two guys, travel to a family cabin. The camera they're using to document the trip keeps glitching out and showing frames of dead bodies in the woods. Suddenly, an apparition drives a knife through one gal's head and then rampages on the other three. But one of these college kids knows more than they're letting on about this undead slasher.

-Return to wraparound: The guy who was left alone with the TVs has vanished, and the corpse is back in his chair. The group from the basement returns and one of them puts in another tape.

-Fourth short: A guy and gal video chat about her new apartment. One night, while they're chatting, a creepy little ghost kid runs in and slams her bedroom door shut. Is it a ghost or something else entirely?

-Return to wraparound: The corpse picks off the intruders one by one.

-Fifth short: A group of guys arrive at a house where they think there's supposed to be a Halloween party, but they instead discover a seance. Ravens fly through the hallways and hands reach through the walls, all trying to prevent their escape.

-Return to wraparound: We don't return to the frame story in the house after this last short, but instead see additional found footage of the Droogs running amok prior to the events in the house. Closing credits roll. It's the music video that producer Brad Miska describes in our Section I interview.

The 2013 sequel, ***V/H/S 2***, has a very similar plot structure as the first film. A group of characters make a tape as they discover and watch other tapes. During the course of the frame story, the tape the main characters are making becomes a part of the collection of tapes they discover.

In the setup, two private investigators are hired to find a missing young man, and inside his house they find a stack of flickering TVs and a whole lot of VHS tapes. As the investigators take turns playing tapes throughout the course of the movie, we watch what they watch.

The shorts include a story of a medical experiment gone wrong in which an eye transplant allows the patient to see things he'd rather not. The next is a particularly brilliant take on the zombie subgenre, in which a GoPro records an afternoon from a zombie's POV. In the third, a documentary crew visits a cult only to find that their superstitions are shockingly real. And the fourth, "Slumber Party Alien Abduction," is, well, exactly what the title suggests. As we return to the frame story between each short, we see the toll the viewing of the tapes has on each character. The progression begins with a simple bloody nose, but culminates in suicide, resurrection, and murder.

The third film, ***V/H/S: Viral***, takes the franchise in a very different direction, as the wraparound style moves away from Found Footage in favor of Film Within A Film. When I spoke to producer Brad Miska about this change he told me this:

> The only thing with the third one, we wanted it to be more polished and add more score type stuff to it. And people were like,

> it's found footage, that doesn't make any sense. Because people don't seem to understand that what they're watching is a mixtape. They're not watching the actual tape of the footage. Somebody made this tape and they're watching the tape that somebody made. So we were just like, let's really break loose with this and do polished shit and break timelines and stuff. It just didn't connect with people…

Nevertheless, ***Viral***'s frame story does tie the series up in a nice bow. We get to learn the reason that all of the tapes we've seen in the trilogy exist, and a clue to their ultimate purpose. As the chaos-causing content goes viral, a literal virus passes over all who come in contact with it. It's a bit ironic that the entry in the trilogy that seems to connect all of the films is also the one that stands apart from the others stylistically. It's a great film, and a great ending to a groundbreaking trilogy.

-The takeaway: One of the things the filmmakers behind ***V/H/S*** do so cleverly is making you feel as though you're watching something that was made just for you rather than a larger audience. It feels individualized, meant for no one else, and that is scary. The characters don't feel like characters, they feel like people. And the tapes seem somehow forbidden.

In this way, whether consciously or unconsciously, the filmmakers are paying homage to the classic anthology

TV series, ***The Outer Limits***. In the introduction to each episode of this show, a voiceover tells us:

> There is nothing wrong with your television set. Do not attempt to adjust the picture. We are controlling transmission. If we wish to make it louder, we will bring up the volume. If we wish to make it softer, we will tune it to a whisper. We will control the horizontal. We will control the vertical. We can roll the image, make it flutter. We can change the focus to a soft blur or sharpen it to crystal clarity. For the next hour, sit quietly and we will control all that you see and hear. We repeat: there is nothing wrong with your television set. You are about to participate in a great adventure. You are about to experience the awe and mystery which reaches from the inner mind to – The Outer Limits.

In truth, there's nothing in this narration that isn't true about any TV show. But it's also deeply individualized, with words like "we," and "you." Phrases like, "mass audience," and "TV sets around the country," are not used, and that is very much deliberate. Highlighting the point, episodes end with a reminder; "We now return control of your television set to you."

Though not stated in as direct a manner as in ***The Outer Limits***, the hyper-reality of the ***V/H/S*** films, the first one in particular, similarly puts the viewer in a place where they lack control; a place where they're seeing something personalized. Is there anything more scary than a horror film made just for you?

• • •

THE ABCS OF DEATH (FILM, 2012)

27 DIRECTORS | RUNTIME: 2HR 9MIN

THE ABCS OF DEATH 2 (FILM, 2014)

31 DIRECTORS | RUNTIME: 2HR 5MIN

THE ABCS OF DEATH 2.5 (FILM, 2016)

32 DIRECTORS | RUNTIME: 1HR 25MIN

-Notable Cast/Crew: Producer Ant Timpson; Writer Simon Barrett; Too many great directors to mention

-Wraparound type: Thematic Throughline, Package Film

-The setup: At the start of the first film a graphic reads:

> The following feature film was created by 26 directors from around the world. Each director was given a letter of the alphabet and asked to choose a word. They then

> created a short tale of death that related to their chosen word. They had complete artistic freedom regarding the content of their segment.

The movie's opening sequence features a house being flooded with blood. In the hallway there are toy blocks, the sort with beveled letters on them, that get caught up and float in the river of blood. At the end of the sequence, the lettered blocks spell out the film's title.

The sequel features a similar setup. This film, however, has different graphical stylings in the introduction and transition pieces. The intro features an animated pop up book that depicts several gruesome scenes come to life, like a girl using a man's intestines as a swing. Instead of the floating blocks motif, the sequel instead shows a skeletal teacher dressed in antique clothes writing on a blackboard.

-A typical short: It would be too much to summarize every short in the three ***ABCs of Death*** features, but of particular interest to me was "C is for Cycle" from the first film. It features a man stuck in a time loop who must deal with his double.

One of my favorite shorts from the second film is from the great indie animator, Bill Plympton. Like most of his work, it's somewhat indescribable. In "H is for Headgames," a man and a woman attack each other with their facial features. Eyelashes become claws, noses become fire hoses, and eyeballs become projectiles. In true

Plympton fashion, the sound design sells the comedy while the animation is grotesque in a predictably unpredictable way. If you're not familiar with his work, be sure to watch this short. You're in for a treat.

-Return to wraparound: At the end of the first ***ABCs*** film, a graphic reads, "Based on a nightmare by Ant Timpson," punctuating the sprawling anthology with a strange sense of cohesion. I enjoyed this final note. It left me thinking about what sort of nightmare might inspire such an ambitious project that involved so many filmmakers.

At the end of the sequel a graphic similarly reads, "Based on a franchise dream by Ant Timpson." I had the chance to ask Ant about this in our Section I interview.

-The takeaway: For ***The ABCs of Death 2***, the producers took submissions for the letter "M" and got over 500 entries. They chose one, "M is for Masticate," to be included in the film, but were left with a plethora of great content. And so, they made ***The ABCs of Death 2.5***, choosing 26 more letter "M" entries to make another feature. The more I thought about this third entry in the ***ABCs*** franchise, the more I realized I could use it as a model for my own efforts.

Early in production of ***Gravedigger Dave's Halfway House***, I decided I'd use the letter "M" approach for my sequel, ***Gravedigger Dave Meets His Match***. I knew I'd want to get the sequel out fast, and soliciting other filmmakers to participate would be the only way to get it done. This is the post I made on FilmFreeway.com:

For the sequel to the anthology film, ***Gravedigger Dave's Halfway House****, we're seeking YOUR shorts! We're looking for genre films of all kinds: horror, docu-horror, sci-fi, haunted house, superhero, supernatural thriller, true crime, and just about anything with a bizarre twist…*

We want to expand the scope of the first film by including shorts from across the globe, as well as including a wider variety of genres. The accepted shorts will be edited into a feature length anthology film screened in Duluth, MN. After the festival, the anthology film will be released to stream globally online for free. It will also be released on DVD and sold at-cost (meaning it will be priced to only cover the costs of manufacturing the DVDs). This is an artistic endeavor only, and the festival will not profit by selling your shorts.

Awards & Prizes

Accepted short films will screen live, edited into the anthology sequel to ***Gravedigger Dave's Halfway House****. Accepted filmmakers will receive "Official Selection" laurels, and be credited as directors. Semi-Finalists aren't being left out, though. The* *concept of this anthology sequel has two characters telling each other stories. As they each struggle to think of the next story to tell, we see them cycle through a variety of stories that appear in the form of rapid flash-frames. This is where the Semi-Finalist films come in. We'll only be showing brief flashes of the semi-finalist films, but we need a ton of content to make the story work. These filmmakers will receive "Semi-Finalist" laurels and be included in the credits and on IMDb as Associate Directors.*

Rules & Terms

By submitting your film you are agreeing to grant nonexclusive rights, which means you are still free to distribute your short film in any way you choose in perpetuity. You are the owner of your film, not us. We only have non-exclusive distribution rights. You can still screen your short at any festival in the world, monetize your short in any way you can, and release your short on YouTube, Vimeo, Prime, television, or anywhere.

While I didn't receive as many submissions as ***ABCs***, ***Gravediggger Dave Meet His Match*** was certainly no slouch, with well over 100 submissions.

CHILLING VISIONS: FIVE SENSES OF FEAR (FILM, 2013)

6 DIRECTORS | RUNTIME: 1HR 28MIN

-Wraparound type: Thematic Throughline, Found Footage

-The setup: This anthology begins with a very creative title sequence in which a guy in a hazmat suit and gas mask both stimulates and tortures a hostage. The torturer sprays perfume in his nose, then sews his nostrils shut; he shines a camera flash right in his eyes and then sews his eyelids shut; he blares music out of huge speakers, then sews his ears shut. The overstimulation, followed by sensory deprivation gives the audience a taste (heh) for what's to come. After the ***Chilling Visions*** title screen, we get a close up shot of the hostage's sewn nose with a "Smell" graphic as we transition into the first short.

-First short: A door-to-door saleswoman forces a bottle of "pheromones" on a down-on-his-luck divorcee, saying they will change his life. After he sprays some on his wrist, the effects are almost immediate. Women notice him, his bosses promote him, and his ex-wife agrees to go on a date with him. But do these social benefits outweigh the horrendous physical effects that slowly begin to manifest? This short revisits a concept that was previously explored in 1993's ***Body Bags***.

-Return to wraparound: Segueing into the next short, we see a close up of the hostage's sewn eyelids with a "See" graphic.

-Second short: An optometrist extracts a fluid from his patients' eyes which he uses as an eyedrop, allowing him to see experiences from his patients' POV. When the optometrist discovers that one of his most coveted patients is being abused by her boyfriend, he takes matters in his own hands.

-Return to wraparound: We see a closeup of the hostage's bound hands with a "Touch" graphic.

-Third short: A blind boy and his parents are in a terrible car crash; one that appears to be caused by a tire trap. When he leaves his injured parents behind to get help, the boy encounters the hideout of a serial killer. There, the two will have a showdown to find out who can outsmart the other. The boy must use his sense of touch if he is to survive. This is the first short to not include a serum of some kind, a fact that will become more important later.

-Return to wraparound: A closeup of the hostage's sewn mouth with a "Taste" graphic.

-Fourth short: A musician is driven via limo to a mysterious office building for a mysterious meeting. While there, he walks by the Avon lady from the "Smell" short and the optometrist from "See," thus establishing the notion that this is all a shared universe. In the meeting, the musician learns they'd like him to write them a song. But when he refuses, the woman interviewing him puts on a set of mechanical teeth and attacks him. Wonderful mayhem ensues.

-Return to wraparound: Wc see a closeup of the hostage's ear, and a "Listen" graphic.

-Fifth short: We cut to full screen text which reads, "The following was received anonymously and may be authentic. Not a single frame has been altered." Accordingly, this short is shot in a found footage style. In this final short, a group of guys and a gal (who also appeared briefly in the "Taste" short) have been tasked with locating a song that is said to kill the listener. Eventually, they piece together bits of info from various sources to locate the mythic song of death. When they do, however, the gal's true motives come to the surface.

-The takeaway: This anthology is an outstanding example of how horror filmmakers can weave interconnectivity between shorts to make a cohesive feature film. Each short stands on it's own and requires no context to be enjoyed, but when they're linked by the wraparound segments the whole thing builds a singular narrative. With this anthology, the whole film is greater than the sum of its parts.

In the sequel, ***Chilling Visions: 5 States of Fear***, each short is centered around a fear: Ego Death, Separation, Mutilation, Extinction, and Loss of Autonomy. You might want to similarly take a broad concept, like senses or fear, and think of how you might divide them into engaging topics for short films. Once you have this, you can try assigning each topic to a filmmaker to make a thematically cohesive anthology. I'm, of course, making it sound much easier than it will be.

ALL HALLOWS' EVE (FILM, 2013)

1 DIRECTOR | RUNTIME: 1HR 23MIN

ALL HALLOWS' EVE 2 (FILM, 2015)

11 DIRECTORS | RUNTIME: 1HR 31MIN

-Notable Cast/Crew: Director Damien Leon

-Wraparound type: Film Within a Film

-The setup: The anthology begins with a babysitter watching over two kids on Halloween night. As they sift through their candy, the boy finds a VHS tape in his bag. Unsure of where it came from, he pleads with the babysitter to let him and his sister watch it.

As they watch the first segment on the tape, the babysitter refers to what they're watching as a short film. She's aware that what she's seeing was made by a film crew, rather than a found footage-style presentation.

-First short: A woman is abducted in a train station by Art the Clown and brought into the tunnels where all manner of demons and devils await. This is the world's first exposure to the Art the Clown of ***The Terrifier***, and he steals the show.

-Return to wraparound: At the conclusion of this short, the babysitter sends the kids to get ready for bed. But we can tell that something is not quite right in the house. When the babysitter sits down to watch ***Dawn of the Dead***, her curiosity gets the better of her, and she puts the tape back in to see what's next.

-Second short: A woman's husband painted a portrait that she keeps covered because of how much it creeps her out. When a UFO lands in the woods outside and it's alien pilot abducts her, the sheet covering the portrait falls and reveals the face to be that of none other than Art the Clown. He proves to be ever-present in this film, even when he's not visible.

-Return to wraparound: The filmmaker drops more hints that the kids and the babysitter aren't the only ones in the house as the babysitter puts the tape in for one more short.

-Third short: Art the Clown terrorizes a girl who stopped for gas at the wrong station, setting him up as an unforgettable horror villain.

-Return to wraparound: At the conclusion of this short, the babysitter receives a call from a frantic woman who claims a clown is trying to kill her. The tape in the VCR continues playing as Art appears to touch the screen from the inside of the TV, trying to get out. She runs upstairs to check on the children, all the while having visions of Art inside the house. What will she find when she gets upstairs? Art never fails to deliver.

-The takeaway: Despite having a very similar wraparound style and structure, the sequel is a departure from the first film in several ways. Gone is the memorable Art the Clown, as is writer/director Damien Leone, who instead served as a producer. He went on to instead write and direct ***The Terrifier***, a non-anthology feature following the exploits of the sadistic Art the Clown. See my Section I interview with Damien for more on how Art the Clown and ***All Hallows' Eve*** came to fruition.

• • •

VOLUMES OF BLOOD (FILM, 2015)

5 DIRECTORS | RUNTIME: 1HR 36MIN

VOLUMES OF BLOOD: HORROR STORIES (FILM, 2016)

6 DIRECTORS | RUNTIME: 1HR 58MIN

-Notable Cast/Crew: Director P.J. Starks

-Wraparound type: Tangential Throughline, Thematic Throughline, Storytelling, Film Within a Film

-The setup: ***Volumes of Blood*** was made in conjunction with a filmmaking program held at a public library, the logistics of which are detailed in my Section I interview with P.J. Starks. The resulting movie is bound together by it's primary framing device of students telling each other stories in a library, a secondary framing device (a Film Within a Film plot twist), and the Thematic Throughline of all segments being shot in the same location. Plot wise, this film feels very Tangential due to its layered framing devices, though for the majority of its runtime it actually does lay out its stories in a traditional Storytelling fashion. The film goes haywire with a fun twist at the end. The sequel, ***Volumes of Blood: Horror Stories***, is the film I've decided to focus on however, as it brings the somewhat tangential nature of the first film to a whole new level.

-The sequel's setup (Wraparound 1): It begins with a short about three crooks who're terrorized by a slasher. A title card pops up reading, "Murder Death Killer," which we then realize is the title of a movie being watched in a packed theater. Two guys start yelling about how much they hate it, until they're kicked out by an employee (who they then chastise).

The two guys in the audience go home and are just about to watch a horror movie on DVD when the theater employee shows up murders one of them. The theater employee then sits down on the couch with the other guy and tells him to press play.

-Next segment (Wraparound 2): We then get a ***Volumes of Blood: Horror Stories*** opening credit sequence, followed by a segment about a slasher going on a Halloween killing spree. So at this point we have seen two films within a film, "Murder Death Killer" in the cinema, and then a DVD, which turns out to be an anthology of its own. The frame story of the DVD centers around a young couple touring a creepy house with a realtor.

-First short: The couple find a creepy mask in a closet and we transition to a short about the origins of the mask that once belonged to a crazed zombie kid.

-Return to wraparound 2: We now go back to the couple touring the house, and when the husband notices blood stains in the bathroom, we transition to a short about that incident.

-Second short: A guy thinks he's gone crazy when he sees the bathtub eating his friends.

-Return to wraparound 2: The couple finds a bloodstained knife in the kitchen.

-Third short: A woman is terrorized by a crazed Christmas caroller who seeks revenge for a Black Friday incident.

-Return to wraparound 2: The realtor insists that the couple see the basement, where there's a huge bloodstain on the floor.

-Fourth short: An older couple gleefully commits murders in the basement, but when a girl breaks free and murders them in self-defense, she's shot in the head by a mysterious masked man.

-Return to wraparound 2: The masked man appears in the basement, murders the house hunters, and goes on a neighborhood murder rampage. Credits roll. But wait. It's not over.

-Return to wraparound 1: Now we go back to the characters watching this anthology DVD: the theater employee and the heckler. The slasher from the DVD is suddenly there, and kills them both. Credits roll again. For real this time.

-The takeaway: This anthology goes down so many tangents that it's plot is difficult to summarize. Some plot points that at first feel unconnected come back around and become relevant, while others don't. This may be the best example of what I think of as a Tangential Throughline anthology.

The plot of this movie is not, of course, meant to be examined as I have done here. It's more like a roller coaster in that every time it turns you can't really remember where you came from, and you certainly have no idea where the next turn will be. The only thing you really know is that you eventually will be heading back to the beginning.

• • •

TALES OF HALLOWEEN (FILM, 2015)

11 DIRECTORS | RUNTIME: 1HR 32MIN

-Notable Cast/Crew: Actor Adrienne Barbeau

-Wraparound type: Thematic Throughline

-The setup: This anthology features a radio broadcaster in a small town on Halloween night who helps transition from short to short. She has a few lines on camera at the start of the film, until it segues to a very imaginative animated title sequence in which we soar above the town and swoop down on frozen scenes from the forthcoming shorts.

-First short: A boy's parents forbid him from eating his Halloween candy with disastrous consequences.

-Second short: Notice there is no return to the wraparound here. The first short ends with a cut to black and then the next short begins with no transition from the DJ. In this short, a boy tries to egg the devil's house, so the devil takes the boy inside and tells him he's going to show the boy the "real" Halloween. The two proceed to go on a path of mayhem and destruction.

-Third short: A group of adults watch movies as trick or treaters come to the door. A group of kids invade their home and start killing them off one by one. But is this really a random act of violence, or are the kids' actions justified?

-Return to wraparound: The DJ comes back with a voiceover about being careful on All Hallow's Eve, as we transition to the next short.

-Fourth short: A teen lures three bullies to the place where they killed his parents so he can enact his revenge.

-Fifth short: When a woman's car breaks down on the way home from a party, she's followed home by the ghost of a disfigured woman.

-Sixth short: A woman transforms into a demon and throws her husband into an oven when he's unable to impregnate her.

-Seventh short: Two neighbors competing for the best Halloween display fight to certain death.

-Return to wraparound: The DJ comes back with warnings of the dangers of Halloween as the next short begins.

-Eighth short: A ***Texas Chainsaw***-style slasher kills a girl. But then an alien inhabits her lifeless corpse and she flies through the air chasing him, screaming like a madwoman. The slasher is terrified, and it's hilarious. Who will be victorious in their final showdown?

-Ninth short: Two thugs kidnap a millionaire's son with plans to hold him for ransom. But their plans go haywire when they realize the son is actually an unkillable goblin.

-Tenth short: A blood-thirsty pumpkin goes on a killing rampage, leading cops on a wild goose chase.

-Return to wraparound: The film concludes with the same animation from the beginning, but now we see it in a whole new context.

-The takeaway: It's the oldest trick in the low budget filmmaking book: hire a horror legend (Adrienne Barbeau) for a single day of easy scenes and intersperse said scenes throughout your entire film. Then, make sure you put her name front and center on the poster. They used this trick in ***Tales of Halloween***, and if you can afford a legendary star for a single day of shooting, you should do it too. It might not be as pricey as you'd expect, and it'll definitely help your film get noticed.

SOUTHBOUND (FILM, 2015)

4 DIRECTORS | RUNTIME: 1HR 29MIN

-Notable Cast/Crew: Producer Brad Miska; Directors Roxanne Benjamin, David Bruckner, & Patrick Horvath

-Wraparound type: Tangential Throughline

-The setup: Two men speed down a desert road, running from some traumatic incident. We're not sure why, but one of them clutches onto a picture of a young girl and seems wracked with guilt. They're pursued by floating demonic apparitions, who chase them to a run-down motel for a bit of psychological torment.

-Next short: At the same motel, three women leave their room, and are followed by the same apparitions (though they don't see them). When their van gets a flat, a strange family offers them a place to stay. But when the family shows some cultish tendencies, one of the women runs off. She's so eager to flag down help that she doesn't hesitate to step out in front of an approaching car. An apparition watches from above.

-Next short: The man in the car is distracted as he talks on the phone, and consequently doesn't see the woman flagging him down for help. He crashes right into her. But he doesn't just leave her there to die on the road. He scoops her up and brings her to a nearby town's medical clinic while 911 dispatch stays on the line with him. The clinic is abandoned, as if it's been the center of a zombie outbreak, so 911 walks him through what he should do to help the woman. But is it really 911 who's on the phone? An apparition watches on.

-Next short: Across the street from the clinic, a woman watches the events of the previous short from a payphone. She hangs up and we follow her to a nearby tavern, where a man barges in, searching for his missing sister. After some mayhem, he is taken to her, but finds her less than welcoming. An apparition watches on.

-Next short: A family is followed as they leave a diner, then attacked at home by men in search of revenge. After an intense home invasion, the attackers are revealed to be the same characters from the setup.

-Return to the setup: We learn that the trauma the men were running from was the home invasion depicted in the previous short. This film is presented nonlinearly, but not just for the sake of it. The characters in this anthology are stuck in a time loop; some sort of perpetual purgatory.

-The takeaway: There's a handoff method used in this anthology that I remember from campfires as a kid. One person would start a scary story, but they wouldn't quite finish it. The person sitting next to them had to pick it up, either adding to it or switching to new characters before passing it along. The story goes around the fire in this fashion until someone decides to end it. As I recall, that's more or less how my favorite campfire story, "Supersonic Radioactive Alien Mutant Space Beavers From Hell," came to be.

It certainly seems that the filmmakers behind ***Southbound*** took a similar approach. One filmmaker starts, but leaves the story open ended for another filmmaker to pick up. In this anthology, each filmmaker sees the previous filmmaker's characters off before introducing a new set of characters. For more details on how this film was made, see my interviews with Producer Brad Miska and actress Maria Olsen in Section I.

• • •

HOLIDAYS (FILM, 2016)

9 DIRECTORS | RUNTIME: 1HR 45MIN

-Notable Cast/Crew: Director Kevin Smith; Actor Seth Green

-Wraparound type: Thematic Throughline

-The setup: In this anthology, each short film takes place on (and is also thematically relevant to) a different holiday. The opening credit sequence reveals a book cover featuring a few iconic holiday symbols: a heart, a clover, mistletoe, and an Easter egg. The book opens, revealing the title of the anthology. The shorts are ordered according to how they fall on the calendar, starting with Valentine's Day.

-First short: A high school girl is bullied for her infatuation with her swim coach. But when she takes revenge on the bullies to impress her crush, how far will she go?

-Return to wraparound: The short ends with an animated greeting reading, “give me your heart,” floating in a sea of black. The card opens and the inside reads “Happy Valentine’s Day.” Every short ends in this fashion.

-Second short: On St. Patrick’s Day, a new girl at school gives her teacher a handmade talisman which impregnates her with a snake monster.

-Third short: On Easter, a little girl wakes up to find a horrifying figure with the head of a rabbit and the body of Jesus Christ lurking in her home.

-Fourth short: On Mother’s Day, a woman is detained by a coven of witches so she can give birth to an unholy demon.

-Fifth short: Next up is Father’s Day, my favorite short in any of the anthologies I’ve ever watched. A woman receives a cassette tape from her father, who she has not seen since childhood. On the tape, he directs her to the last place they saw each other so that they may be reunited. But what are his true intentions, and what is the true nature of the place to which she’s being led?

-Sixth short: Directed by the renowned Kevin Smith, the Halloween short shows what happens when the head of a porn ring denies women the right to celebrate the holiday.

-Seventh short: Seth Green, the mind behind the brilliant comedy anthology ***Robot Chicken***, stars in the Christmas short. His character is sent by his wife to get the most coveted gift of the year for their son, a pair of VR specs that show the user their true selves. But when the last pair are snatched up right before he can get to them, he'll go to insane lengths to appease his family.

-Eighth short: On New Year's Eve, a serial murderer plots to kill his date, but when she turns out to have some twisted tendencies of her own, the nature of their date quickly changes.

-The takeaway: I'm not using hyperbole when I write that "Father's Day" is my favorite short film of all time. The acting is great, the suspense kills me, and the way it uses sound design to evoke the protagonist's childhood is masterfully executed. I've watched this short many times, and it continues to inspire me.

• • •

PATIENT SEVEN (FILM, 2016)

9 DIRECTORS | RUNTIME: 1HR 56MIN

-Notable Cast/Crew: Actors Michael Ironside, Amy Smart, & Doug Jones; Director Nicholas Peterson

-Wraparound type: Storytelling

-The takeaway: This film features a setup that's somewhat reminiscent of ***Asylum.*** Michael Ironside plays a psychiatrist who visits an institution to research patients for a book he's writing. He wants to determine whether the patients he's selected to interview are actually mentally ill, or are merely faking it to divert attention away from their heinous crimes.

He interviews a twenty-seven year old patient who's been institutionalized since she was ten. After some violent coercion, she tells him the tale that led her to this awful place.

-First short: This short flashes back to when she was a child. Her mother believes their family is being haunted by a demon, but the actions she takes to defend her daughter may cause more harm than good. (For more on this short and the way ***Patient Seven*** was put together, see my interview with director Nicholas Peterson in Section I.)

-Return to wraparound: After interviews with several more patients, we return to the wraparound segment to learn that the doctor is, in fact, also a patient in the asylum.

-Final short: It turns out that Ironside's family was attacked by zombies, but instead of allowing them to become infected, he, as a child, beats them to death with a tire iron; a mercy killing that would never be understood by a jury.

-Return to wraparound: Now that we know his backstory, Ironside's character storms off to take control of the institution.

-The takeaway: This anthology featured shorts that were acquired to fit the wraparound, rather than produced for the wraparound. To make the shorts fit into the wraparound, the anthology's producers cleverly made each short a flashback. If you plan on including pre-made shorts in your anthology, definitely consider ***Patient Seven***'s approach in tying them all together. It's certainly easier than having to track down and rehire the actors from each and every short.

• • •

XX (FILM, 2017)

5 DIRECTORS | RUNTIME: 1HR 32MIN

-Notable Cast/Crew: Directors Sofia Carrillo & Roxanne Benjamin

-Wraparound type: Thematic Throughline

-The setup: The anthology begins with a creepy stop motion animation segment. We move through a decrepit playroom that has a dollhouse placed atop a four-legged end table. A disembodied doll's head slides out of the front door and opens an end table drawer, revealing pearls arranged to display the anthology's title, ***XX***. The front of the dollhouse features a circular face on a swivel that can spin to look within or peer outside of the house. It's bizarre, surreal, and invites many interpretations.

-First short: On a train, a strange man shows a boy the contents of a beautiful red box, which somehow leads to the boy's abrupt self-starvation. How will the mother cope with her son's mysterious affliction as it spreads to her whole family and her life begins to unravel?

-Return to wraparound: The dollhouse uses the four legs of the end table to walk out of the playroom and explore the house. A locust enters the front door of the dollhouse and crawls down a dark tunnel. The face on the front of the dollhouse dabs her mouth with a cloth, signifying she's eaten the locust, and providing a roundabout commentary on the first short.

-Second short: This one is pretty hilarious. A mother goes to great lengths to hide the fact that her husband has died at home just before their daughter's birthday party.

-Return to wraparound: A pincushion represents the dollhouse's lungs. Objects are slowly sewn into the cushion, including a tooth, two small fingers, and a cloth with an embroidered "M." The meaning here goes right over my head. Perhaps there is no intended meaning, but the viewer is nevertheless free to assign their own symbolism to these bizarre vignettes.

-Third short: Four friends embark on a desert camping trip and find primitive cave drawings on a rocky surface that foreshadows the remainder of their disastrous trip.

-Return to wraparound: An apple represents the dollhouse's heart, which quickly turns black and rots, perhaps a commentary on the final fate of the previous short's main character.

-Fourth short: A mother fears what might become of her son as he turns 18 and confronts his demonic destiny.

-Return to wraparound: The dollhouse puts a dead bird into a doll's chest, giving the doll life. The dollhouse then comes upon a lifeless child with a strange door built into her chest. The dollhouse puts the dead bird inside the door and closes it, giving life to the girl. The dollhouse and the girl gaze into each other's eyes as the anthology comes to a close.

-The takeaway: This movie's wraparound certainly invites varying interpretations. As anthologies may be viewed as films within a film, featuring narratives within narratives, so is this dollhouse a house within a house, with the ability to look both within and outside of herself. Viewed from this perspective, the playroom becomes an analogy for an anthology's wraparound, while the inside of the dollhouse becomes analogous to the smaller, more confined short films. Of course this analogy seems far fetched, but this is the most abstract frame story I've come across in my examination of horror anthologies. Most are very direct in their purpose, and of course there's nothing wrong with that. But if you've been looking for a more experimental approach, ***XX*** may be your anthology of choice. Wraparound director Sofia Carrillo gave me the background on how this wraparound came to be in our Section I interview.

THE DARK TAPES (FILM, 2017)

2 DIRECTORS | RUNTIME: 1HR 38MIN

-Notable Cast/Crew: Director Michael McQuown

-Wraparound type: Found Footage, Tangential Through-line

-The setup (Wraparound 1): As this is a found footage anthology, each segment has a slate identifying the tape. The first reads, "The Dark Tapes, Tape #100, Discovering Dark Tape #01, Year:2007." A man and a woman enter their community theater to find the set has been wrecked. They also discover a camcorder that's recording them. This scene serves as an introductory framing device, as the audience will learn thc origins of the camcorder and the wrecked set over the course of the next segment, which serves as a secondary wraparound.

-Next segment (Wraparound 2): "Dark Tape #01 Part A, To Catch a Demon, Year: 2007." Two men and a woman enter the same community theater, prior to its eventual damage, to conduct a sleep experiment. They discuss demons, and how such "trans-dimensional entities" may become visible to a person who enters REM sleep. Demons exist in a time-plane that humans cannot perceive when awake. But some can in REM sleep, which explains the existence of night terrors.

-First short: "Dark Tape #02, The Hunters and the Hunted, Year: 2011." A couple moves into a house and recruits a team of paranormal investigators when they witness slamming doors and mysterious footsteps. But does the couple know more about this phenomenon than they're letting on? Is there something more sinister than a ghost at work?

-Return to wraparound 2: We go back to "Dark Tape 01." The group in the theater records a man sleeping in hopes they can catch a glimpse of a demon when he enters REM sleep. As the man is prone to night terrors, they are able to make contact. The demon says, "He is with me. He has always been with me. We are eternal."

-Second short: "Dark Tape #03, Cam Girls, Year: 2013." Here, two women lure a man to what they promise will be a private sex show, only to reveal that one of them is a demon, the other is the demon's servant, and that the man is in store for something much different than what he expected.

-Return to wraparound 2: The characters conducting the sleep study in "Dark Tape 01" realize they've been transported to the demon's dimension, effectively making them ghosts, as they try to get back to the real world while something sinister approaches.

-Third short: "Dark Tape #04, Amanda's Revenge, Year: 2015." This segment begins with a woman saying that she knows how to defeat her captors. Then we go back four months, to a party where she's drugged. Although her friends are able to save her from being attacked, they aren't able to save her from the demonic possession that immediately follows.

-Return to wraparound 2: When we return to the sleep experiment in the theater, the anthology begins to come full circle in a way somewhat reminiscent of a Christopher Nolan film. Things go haywire for the group stuck in the alternate timestream (which is inhabited by all manner of demons and monsters). The woman makes it back to what appears to be the real world. But, looks can be deceiving.

-Return to wraparound 1: Now we come to the point where the two narratives that frame this anthology come together. As it happens, the woman from the sleep experiment is still caught in the demon's dimension, which has a much faster time dilation than we humans are accustomed to. While she moves at normal speed, it appears to her that the folks discovering the trashed theater aren't moving at all. Likewise, the folks discovering the trashed theater cannot perceive her because she's moving too fast for them to register. It ties up the entire anthology in an extremely clever time paradox.

-The takeaway: When the anthology loops back to the beginning, reshowing us the first scene of the movie in an entirely new context, it gives the non-linear plot a purpose. It isn't just nonlinear for the sake of being clever. It's nonlinear because the subject matter supports such a plot structure, and visa versa. And that's what I love most about this anthology. For more on this film's plot, see my Section I interview with director Michael McQuown.

CREEPED OUT (SERIES, 2017-CURRENT)

23 EPISODES | EPISODE RUNTIME: ~30MIN

-Notable Cast/Crew: Co-creators Bede Blake & Robert Butler

-Wraparound type: Thematic Throughline

-The setup: This anthology series features cautionary tales for kids about the dangers of popularity, bullying, and self-absorption. The frame story for each episode involves a mysterious masked figure, The Curious, who travels around looking for creepy tales. He appears at the beginning and end of each episode, his scenes voiced over by a female narrator who tells us, "If you hear his whistle, you know that something creepy is about to happen."

-A typical episode: From there we transition to isolated tales that often end unhappily for the main character. In one episode, a girl recites a spell given to her by a puppet that will grant her absolute control over her embarrassing parents. In another, a babysitter scares kids into going to bed early to impress a boy she likes, until the tables are turned by one little hell raiser. In another, a boy who trolls his friends online must act quickly when he starts morphing into an actual troll.

-Return to wraparound: Episodes often return to the frame story when the protagonist has learned his lesson, but we get the sense that there is more to each episode's tale that we don't get to see. This, apparently, is all of the story that The Curious feels he needs to witness, and nothing more. So he moves on.

-The takeaway: This show feels very much like a continuation of ***Are you Afraid of the Dark?*** and ***Goosebumps***. Fans of these shows definitely need to check it out. Co-creator Bede Blake talks more about this in our Section 1 interview.

• • •

THE FIELD GUIDE TO EVIL (FILM, 2018)

9 DIRECTORS | RUNTIME: 1HR 57MIN

-Notable Cast/Crew: Producer Ant Timpson

-Wraparound type: Thematic

-The setup: At the time of my correspondence with producer Ant Timpson about ***The ABCs of Death***, I had not yet seen, ***The Field Guide to Evil***. I did ask him if he hoped to do something different than the ***ABCs*** franchise. He told me, "Definitely wanted to do something with global folklore for a long time and wanted to focus the content. If ***ABCs*** was an old circus, ***The Field Guide to Evil*** is like the Alligator Man exhibit." His statement definitely had me ready to watch something quite different than what I had seen before in his films, as I was not disappointed.

This film begins with an animated open depicting scenes from the lore-inspired shorts we're about to see. We then transition to a storybook motif often seen in anthology films, such as the Cohen Brothers' film from the previous year, ***The Ballad of Buster Scruggs***. In ***The Field Guide to Evil***, each short begins with a closeup of text from the book, giving us some context, including the short's country of origin and a blurb about the lore that inspired it.

-First short: In this period piece, a young woman is subjected to a cruel bout of paranormal conversion therapy as punishment for her secret love with another woman. It becomes apparent early in this short that, despite having the same producers, this film is quite different from the ***ABCs*** franchise. In terms of style and pacing, it feels much more akin to the 2015 period piece ***The VVitch*** than anything else.

-Second short: A new mother must fight the demonic forces that threaten her baby, and her sanity.

-Third short: A man traveling through the woods is transfixed by a demonic woman who promises him limitless knowledge if he consumes three human hearts. So he naturally takes up grave robbing.

-Fourth short: A vacationing family of three is terrorized by a group of cannibal kids with oversized heads.

-Fifth short: When a goblin attempts to disguise himself so he can partake in drunken holiday festivities, an entire village turns against him.

-Sixth short: A group of explorers travel to an ancient temple in India in search of relics they can sell to the circus. That is, until they lay eyes on a forbidden sight no human is meant to see. Stylistically, this short is reminiscent of Jacques Cousteau's nature documentaries.

-Seventh short: A brother and sister living together in the 1700s are plagued by a diseased rodent that makes its home in the sister's mouth.

-Eighth short: In this final short, two fraternal shoemakers betray each other for the love of a beautiful princess.

-The takeaway: After this last short, the film's closing credits roll without returning to the linking device of the floating book. This reminds me of the Boris Karloff-hosted anthology, ***Black Sabbath***, which does not return to the host after the final short. While it does nothing to the quality of the anthology to not wrap everything up prior to the closing credits, I tend to prefer a bow to be tied around everything. The anthology, ***60 Seconds to Die***, does a good job of reinforcing a sense of cohesion between the short films in its final moments. There's no right or wrong here, but be sure to consider what approach is more in-line with your sensibilities.

GHOST STORIES (FILM, 2018)

2 DIRECTORS | RUNTIME: 1HR 38MIN

-Notable Cast/Crew: Writer/Director/Producer/Star Andy Nyman; Writer/Director/Producer Jeremy Dyson; Actor Martin Freeman

-Wraparound type: Storytelling

-The setup: This anthology begins by introducing us to Phillip Goodman, who has made it his life's work to debunk fraudulent paranormal investigators. When he's called to the home of one of the experts in his field, Goodman's sense of purpose is turned upside down. The expert has encountered three cases which have made him begin to accept the paranormal. Sick and nearing the end of his life, he tasks Goodman with investigating the three cases for himself. He pleads with Goodman, "Tell me I'm wrong."

-First short: Goodman meets the first storyteller at a pub, and must offer payment to hear the story. This man, a nightwatchman, is plagued by unexplainable power outages, misplaced objects, malfunctioning radios, and visions of a young girl.

-Return to wraparound: We're suddenly at a church, where Goodman is already interviewing the nightwatchman's priest, who insists that the validity of the story should be judged not by the material evidence, but by how the nightwatchman's life improved after the incident.

Goodman leaves to interview the next subject, a teenage boy. But all is not well within this house. The boy's parents stare at a wall lifelessly, doors slam, images of demons are pinned all over, and there are an abundance of locks on the doors. When the teen begins telling his story, it sheds more light on these peculiarities.

-Second short: In his story, the teen is driving down a lonely stretch of road, arguing with his parents on the phone. Distracted, he hits a goat-headed devil with his car. He tries to drive off and pretend it didn't happen, but this devil has other ideas.

-Return to wraparound: Goodman visits the woods where the teen had this encounter, speaking into a tape recorder about how the mind sees what it wants to see, until he is shaken by a vision of his own corpse in the driver's seat of his car.

We cut to Goodman and the third subject walking through the countryside as the latter recounts the story of his wife getting pregnant. Here, a very creative technique is used to transition to the third short. This third storyteller, Priddle, says he dropped his wife off at a clinic after she began having trouble with the pregnancy, and then returned home to do some work. Goodman asks, "What time was that?" Before Priddle can answer, the filmmakers abruptly cut to the short, where Priddle notes the time aloud. I haven't seen this question/answer technique used in any other horror anthology, and its effect is perfect, bringing the audience from one segment to another before they even realize there's been a change.

-Third short: Priddle is tidying up around the nursery when objects begin to move around without explanation.

We return to the frame story, where Goodman and Priddle discuss poltergeists, and then return to the short. This crosscutting between short and wraparound is fairly uncommon in anthologies, but can also be found in 1986's ***Deadtime Stories***.

-Return to wraparound: Without spoiling too many details (I want you to watch ***Ghost Stories*** for yourself) this is where the movie kicks into high gear. The conclusion of this film defies expectations as it ventures into the surreal. What transpires is operatic in its grandeur and unsettling in its strangeness. As it reaches the twist, you'll remember all of the hints dropped in throughout. Shots, scenes, and characters that seemed out of place early in the film suddenly begin to fit. I won't spoil any more than that.

-The takeaway: The unconventional way in which this movie jumps from segment to segment makes it a truly engaging watch for those well acquainted with the horror anthology subgenre. It truly feels like a singular vision rather than a bunch of shorts that were piecemealed together. Andy Nyman and I talk about how the film was assembled in our Section I interview.

GRAVEDIGGER DAVE'S HALFWAY HOUSE (FILM, 2020)

1 DIRECTOR | RUNTIME: 1HR 12MIN

-Notable Cast/Crew: Actor Matt Rasmussen; Director Keith Tyler Hopkins

-Wraparound type: Storytelling

-The setup: In a bizarre sort of infomercial, Gravedigger Dave introduces himself to the audience as the keeper of a post-hospice for the undead. A girl arrives at the Halfway House, dead from a cause we're never told, and wielding a hatchet that's bloody for reasons we'll never learn. Gravedigger Dave is about to banish her to hell, but has a sudden change of heart. He'd feel bad sending someone so young into the fire, so he makes a deal with her. He's going to tell her a series of spooky stories, and if she can tell him which are true and which he's made up, then he'll reassign her to earth. The girl agrees to the terms of the deal, and Gravedigger Dave begins telling her the first story.

-First short: Originally titled, ***Take Your Non-Vaporous Apparition to Work Day***, this short takes a comedic look at a ghost following a man around the office as he tries to wrap up his day.

-Return to wraparound: The girl doesn't believe the story is true, but Gravedigger Dave did start with an easy one. They won't all be so cut and dry.

-Seconds short: A woman invites a camera crew to document something strange going on in her home.

-Return to wraparound: Gravedigger Dave tells the girl not to judge each story as he tells it, but to wait until all the stories have been told. Then he asks if she's ever heard of a paranormal investigator.

-Third short: A team of paranormal investigators explore an abandoned asylum and an old shipping vessel.

-Return to wraparound: Gravedigger Dave begins the story of a ghost hunter who wrote a book about his experiences.

-Fourth short: The ghost hunter recounts an investigation he conducted at a haunted Greyhound bus museum.

-Return to wraparound: Gravedigger Dave tells the girl that some folks don't realize until it's too late that they should've called ghost hunters to investigate a paranormal incident.

-Fifth short: A handyman is haunted by a possessed portrait as he works to restore a derelict house.

-Return to wraparound: Gravedigger Dave tells the girl that while some people unintentionally awaken paranormal forces, others do it with malicious intent.

-Sixth short: A deranged woman finds a typewriter with an UNDO key, allowing her to undo the last action she took prior to pressing the button. As her experiments with the typewriter become more and more extreme, she learns that it only has a finite number of undos to give to her.

-Return to wraparound: Almost admitting that the previous story was made up, Gravedigger Dave tells the girl he has a story that's a bit more grounded.

-Seventh short: A woman remembers the ghost that cut her throat in the middle of the night as she slept.

-Return to wraparound: Gravedigger Dave tells the girl that when it comes to true tales of the paranormal, certain nonbelievers may influence the way in which the story is told.

-Eighth short: A woman remembers the ghosts that haunt the children she works with.

-Return to wraparound: Gravedigger Dave takes interest in how some people may want the location of a paranormal incident to remain undisclosed. Luckily, that isn't the case with his next story.

-Ninth short: The ghost of a young girl haunts a railroad museum. She even makes an appearance in a wedding photo taken in the museum's Great Hall many years ago.

-Return to wraparound: Gravedigger Dave muses about how certain locations seem to be a beacon for paranormal activity.

-Tenth Short: A ghost at a restored theater has a penchant for stealing doorstops.

-Return to wraparound: Gravedigger Dave says that the incident at the theater was "probably" a ghost. He tells the girl to keep that in mind as she listens to the final story.

-Eleventh short: The author of ***Haunted Lakes*** considers it to be rather unimportant whether a given ghost story is "true." What matters is that ghost stories are a part of our history and heritage.

-Return to wraparound: Gravedigger Dave tells the girl that, for the fate of her soul, she must tell him which stories were true, and which were made up. She interrupts him, insisting that all stories are both true and untrue because it's all up to the listener. But has she passed Gravedigger Dave's test?

-The takeaway: I found ***Lore*** extremely helpful as I entered preproduction on ***Gravedigger Dave's Halfway House***. It gave me incredible insight on how I might blend documentary scenes with narrative scenes. I also spent a lot of time watching ***Unsolved Mysteries*** for inspiration on how to weave horror elements into documentary segments. My framing device, though, would differ in an essential way from these shows. I wanted to create a character that was a hybrid between The Cryptkeeper and Ernest P. Worrell. I don't think there's an actor on the planet besides Matt Rasmussen that could've pulled it off with such charisma. For details on how I was able to get this weird little anthology film funded, continue on to Section III.

SECTION III: THE TAKEAWAY

(FINAL THOUGHTS AND INSPIRATION)

In June of 2018, before beginning work on this book, I applied for a $10,000 grant with the Minnesota State Arts Board to complete a paranormal anthology film. I've included excerpts from my grant application below so you can see how one anthology film was able to obtain its funding. First though, I ought to add that when I initially aspired to make an anthology out of my short films, I never imagined that the project would take the shape that you'll read about. I knew going into the application process that I couldn't just make a generic horror film. There had to be some societal or cultural benefit to the State of Minnesota, otherwise there'd be no way the State of Minnesota would give me the money. With the help of a great screenwriter, great editor, and great friend by the name of Matthew Dressel, I came to a concept that would suit my desire to make a series of paranormal shorts, but also would document Minnesota's folklore. It may sound like I compromised to get the money, but that couldn't be further from the truth. In fact, the process of making my project grant-worthy actually helped me uncover a whole new realm of storytelling possibilities that I'd never have thought of otherwise. With that in mind, here are excerpts from my narrative. I hope it'll give you ideas on how to fund your project.

GRAVEDIGGER DAVE'S GRANT PROPOSAL

Artist's Plan

Filmmaker Keith Hopkins will complete a feature film that will explore St. Louis County ghost stories and folklore with the help of local historians and paranormal enthusiasts.

Artist's Background

My paranormal short films include, ***Boots****,* ***Stray****,* ***Undo****,* ***Take Your Non-Vaporous Apparition to Work Day****, and* ***Gravedigger Dave's Halfway House****. Directing these films was an invaluable learning experience, and they all have given me the opportunity to explore narrative storytelling and ghost stories from a different angle. After gaining feedback from collaborators and audiences at public screenings, I'm proud to write that each one has been a technical and stylistic improvement on the previous.*

My most recent project, the documentary series, ***Night at the Armory****, explored the historic Duluth Armory's storied past and featured performances by local musicians like Charlie Parr and Superior Siren. The goal was to seamlessly blend entertainment and local history, with the musical performances serving as segue pieces between historical segments. This drew an incredibly diverse audience, ranging from* *young people who wanted to see local bands play in an abandoned building, to senior members of the Duluth community who remember the glory days of the Armory.*

In my proposed film, ***Gravedigger Dave's Halfway House****, I will combine what I've learned from both paranormal and documentary filmmaking to once again blend entertainment and local history. I will conduct interviews with Ken Buehler, a historian from the Duluth Depot, and members of the Duluth Paranormal Society to gain knowledge of regional ghost stories and folklore. Afterwards, I will construct narrative vignettes that explore St. Louis County's folklore, with my original character, Gravedigger Dave, serving as the host. This character will give the audience context and function as a segue device between vignettes, similar to the way the musicians functioned as segue devices between historical segments in* ***Night at the Armory****. I am confident my artistic background has laid the groundwork to successfully complete* ***Gravedigger Dave's Halfway House****.*

IMPACT ON THE CREATIVE COMMUNITY

The intended audience consists of members of St. Louis County who have an interest in local history but aren't familiar with regional ghost stories. I expect a diverse age range in the audience, similar to the diverse audience I was able to engage with ***Night at***

***the Armory**.*

*After **Night at the Armory** screenings, many viewers said there was much about the building's history they knew nothing about. Even more gratifying than that, Mark Poier of the Armory Arts and Music Center has told me that my documentary has brought awareness to their cause of revitalizing the historic structure. I'm proud that my work has played a part in the effort to preserve local history, and **Gravedigger Dave's Halfway House** will likewise encourage such preservation.*

*The production of **Gravedigger Dave's Halfway House** will bring me to historic sites in St Louis County, some of which have histories that are not widely known. By bringing awareness to such places and stories, I'll once again be able to inspire the preservation of local history. This feature film will serve as a means of cataloging history and inspiring my audience to preserve their local folklore for future generations in a way that no other film has attempted. If people are to remember their local history, they need works of art to carry that history forward.*

• • •

Holy crap was I over the moon when I heard my grant proposal had been approved. In the grand scheme of feature filmmaking, $10,000 is essentially nothing. But as a weekend warrior, with 13ish years experience in TV and some very talented friends, $10,000 can go a long way. I was well-positioned to make this film on the cheap.

Budget-wise, I allocated the grant towards equipment purchase, payment to my lead actor Matt Rasmussen, payment to myself for editing time (as I'd have to turn down freelance work to make the feature), marketing expenses for the movie's premier, and craft services during the shoots.

I was intimidated by the prospect of having to release the movie one year after receiving the funds, but the words of wisdom you'll read next helped me keep my head above water.

WORDS OF WISDOM

While prepping my wraparound segments for production, I began to wonder who else was out there making anthology films. I started posting on social media sites looking for anthology filmmakers who'd be willing to do an interview with me.

I had no idea how many indie anthologies were being made. It was crazy! What follows are some great pieces of advice from some wonderful filmmakers. All seem to find great value in anthology filmmaking for the collaborative experience, as well as for the potential of increased exposure. They also shared some words of caution. I hope you can learn a lot from them. I sure did.

• • •

PAUL WENNERSBERG-LØVHOLEN

(GRINDSPLOITATION SUPERVISING PRODUCER)

I wrote a hell of a lot of feature scripts and even sent a couple to Troma (without success), had a few disastrous film shoots where I blew a lot of time and money on failed features, before finally coming into the fold around 2005 when I volunteered with Troma at the Cannes Film Festival. I ended up working 3 successive years at Cannes and got to know Troma and Lloyd Kaufman (almost) intimately… It can be quite scary for filmmakers to have to sign away all the rights to their film but unfortunately that's how it is. Therefore it's important that filmmakers know who they are working with, what is going to become of the film and bring up any questions, concerns or clauses that they would like in the contract, before they give their child away. There are some horror stories out there of artists being misled, or signing away all the rights only for an anthology to just die a death and never see the light of day, with all the shorts then stuck in a legal limbo...

Before you even shoot a second of film, it's essential to have everyone involved sign a release. It happens a lot that cast or crew suddenly have a change of heart, falling out, or go on some ego power trip with the director involved, refusing to sign a release when a film has reached completion. Or an actor can disappear or even die post shoot (we had that with one short on ***Grindsploitation***). Just one little signature, from one person who may have the tiniest of parts in your film, can land your project in jeopardy and result in it never being distributed. All the major, and reputable, producers and distributors will ask for these releases so be prepared and get that John Hancock on the paper on day one. As to why they should be involved in anthologies, I think that for people that like working with this medium, that being shorts as opposed to features (though many filmmakers I know dabble in both), it's a fantastic way of finding an outlet for your films. It's also great to collaborate with other artists and see what, together, you can achieve.

DAN BROWNLIE

(THREE'S A SHROUD EXECUTIVE PRODUCER)

The Modern Indie Horror Anthology (a blessing and a curse). Putting together any film let alone indie film is a pitfall of stress, troubles and leaving yourself open to being messed around. When working on an anthology with multiple directors this just multiplies. You're not only handling the stress of your film you are also taking on the stress of the other directors too as you have to balance their budgets, deliverables and making sure it is all on time.

Whether they are good quality or not the modern indie horror anthology does have its place, it gives people IMDb credits and an ego boost (two things that can completely turn a new director's day around). The things to make sure of whether you're putting your own anthology together or working on someone else's just make sure you have everything legally covered. People signed off, soundtrack signed off, location signed off, any friends working on it get them signed off (I even get my wife to sign release forms when we've worked on shorts) and for god's sake be so careful of who you distribute to. Out of the seven anthologies (two of which I produced in full) I have not seen a penny off any of them. If you just want your film out there then distribute it to the hell you want, if it's just a circulating film to get you out there then there are plenty of people who will get it out there. But if you want any form of return on your investment then get yourself a sales agent and do a ton of research. Overall anthologies are fun and a fun way of getting you going in the world of film, just tread exceptionally carefully and make sure you know what you want from it.

• • •

MICHAEL J. EPSTEIN

(60 SECONDS TO DIE DIRECTOR)

Anthologies are extremely popular at the moment, and many are wide open for unsolicited submissions. Take a look at the companies and producers making them and just reach out to them to find out more. Most importantly, make the best films you can and producers will come to you! Now that I have worked with many of the producers involved in creating these anthologies, I get inquiries to be involved with new ones on a regular basis. They need content! If you can make good content, you'll be in demand!

IAN FISCHER

(SHORT FILM FEATURED IN TROMA DANCE & WORLD OF DEATH)

Lack of knowledge does not excuse lack of action. So I handed out VHS copies [of the short film "Foet"] at the 2000 San Diego Comic Con. One guy who took a copy was Mr. Lloyd Kaufman himself. Mr Toxic Avenger. The Troma guy. I was floored when he emailed or called me and told me he wanted to show it at Tromadance in Park-Fucking-City during Sundance… Eventually, the contract with Troma lapsed (and they followed the common Distributor "lost the paperwork" M.O.- so they kept it for years after the contract lapsed). But, I feel very loyal to Lloyd for believing in me when people despised it. So what's a couple of extra years and missing quarterly earning reports between friends?

I think horror anthologies work the best out of all the different genres. The ***V/H/S*** series, ***ABCs of Death*** series, ***XX***, ***Southbound***, and P.J. Starks' ***Volumes of Blood*** series kickass. But here is the thing, short films are easily viewed on YouTube and Vimeo. Why would a new filmmaker want to be in an anthology? I think there are three reasons, and any one of them are valid.

> **1)** Money. Can you profit from inclusion in an anthology more than on your own? Does making money even matter to you? Some filmmakers just have fun and that's the point for them.

> **2)** Exposure. Will your work reach a larger audience through a built in audience (like Troma) or from the other filmmakers' fanbase?... Filmmaking is too tough to make a short and just leave it sitting on a shelf.
> **3)** Bragging rights. Don't underestimate the cool factor in telling your friends, boss, Uber driver, first date, or bootie call that your film is available for purchase.

If numbers 1-3 don't interest you, just release your short film yourself. Build your audience. Hell, it's pretty common for filmmakers to put out anthologies full of their own work.

• • •

MJ DIXON

(GRINDSPLOITATION DIRECTOR)

Just try and get a clear idea of what they plan to do. I've been approached dozens of times to contribute to anthologies, and it's very rare that I get involved unless I feel it's on the level. There's a trend growing just throwing content out there and seeing what sticks and using other filmmakers to make up that run time, it's becoming a large part of indie film, so it's worth being careful and selective. I think it becomes obvious when someone is just trying to make a quick buck off your content without doing any work and some people build entire filmographies by using other peoples films. It's important that you know where you stand with your work and what will happen to it. If you're making something, then you want to know that it's going to see the light of day, so it's definitely a good idea to make sure that you keep the rights to your films if you're not receiving anything upfront.

• • •

MAUDE MICHAUD

(WOMEN IN HORROR MONTH BLOOD DRIVE PSA DIRECTOR)

Just keep making films and try to get your work out there as much as possible. You're gonna fail, but it doesn't matter. Don't dwell on it, learn from your mistakes, pick yourself up and start again. Always try to do the best you can with the resources you have access to and turn your limitations into creative challenge. If your budget is limited or don't have access to practical effects, try to think of another story that can be done with what you have access to and that is as effective. I'm not gonna lie, it's really hard and competition is fierce, so you have to really want it/be passionate about it and always keep at it.

And respect the theme/topic! It might be super tempting to try to bend the rules, but anthology projects are so hard to market, the content needs to be 100% relevant and the best it can be. So, keep your cool experimentation ideas for your own short and instead show people how creative you can be within the theme! That's the best way to stand out and have your work be noticed. I've personally always seen anthology projects as the best way to challenge my creativity and really push it! Oh and have fun with it! If you make a project you don't really care about just for the sake of making something, it will show, trust me.

• • •

PETE YAGMIN

(60 SECONDS TO DIE DIRECTOR)

Don't be afraid to experiment and transcend genres! And if you're someone who thrives on challenges - anthologies are a great way to try something new, perhaps with a theme or idea that is typically outside your wheelhouse. The only way to grow is to step outside your comfort zone.

CHRIS AMBRIZ

(DIRECTOR OF MUERTE: TALES OF HORROR)

Be passionate about the stories you are telling, no top notch camera or editing software is going to make a lack of story any better… Surround yourselves with people that want to support you and your vision. Avoid people that just want to tell you want you want to hear and not tell you the truth or back out at the last minute. And if you want a better chance at a distribution deal but don't have a full feature idea, an anthology can give you a chance to really cut your teeth on different horror subjects and still get you in feature length size. But a good "wraparound concept" is key to making a good anthology, anybody can butt together short films in a timeline, but coming up with a clever way to tie them together is the real goal when making an anthology horror film.

• • •

MIKE WATT

(WRITER OF MOVIE OUTLAW)

I've watched scores of movies that couldn't live up to what the wraparound promised. I like Paul Talbot's indie anthologies - ***Hellblock 13***, ***Freakshow***, ***Cremains*** - because the stories are on-par with the set-up, albeit hampered, as usual, by lower budget. ***Tales of Poe*** doesn't have any wrap-around and lets the stories speak for themselves. Ultimately, the key to any anthology, as with any movie, lies more in the writing and less in the execution. A great script will bear low production values. As we've witnessed time and again by the studios, the opposite does NOT hold true. A good script is the cheapest part of your production and should take the most amount of time to get right.

We need to get away from the EC brand of "twist ending" shorts. Study the form, get it down, then figure out new ways to present the material, because after ***Twilight Zone***, ***Outer Limits***, ***Tales from the Crypt***, the "twist" is expected and we can see it coming now. You have thousands of years of literature and storytelling at your disposal. Study the short-story format, figure out how to make that work on screen again.

The Amicus anthologies are your high water mark, but they're also where most people start AND stop. Once you get through them all and land on ***Torture Garden***, you should be able to figure out what works and what doesn't. Again, don't rely strictly on movies to show you how to tell a story. Go back to classic literature - study Poe and Maupassant, du Maurier, Fredrick Brown (a master of the two-page short story). All your heroes were influenced by the classics, you should be too.

FINAL THOUGHTS

I'm happy to report that this book, for me anyway, was a success. I had set out to glean something, anything, from those who'd come before me as I crafted ***Gravedigger Dave's Halfway House***. If I've learned anything about filmmaking it's that an anthology should be greater than the sum of its shorts. When a collection of shorts is stronger than the shorts would have been individually, it's my opinion that the anthology has succeeded.

There are so many filmmakers in the world who, like yourself, are gunning for the elusive feature. I sincerely hope this book has given you some ideas on how to achieve that goal. So go now. Make awesome shorts. Think hard about a wraparound. And most importantly, have fun.

ACKNOWLEDGEMENTS

A million thanks to Mom, Maria, Olivia, and Christine, who always support and believe in me; Dad, who was the best campfire storyteller ever; Matthew Dressel, who always pushes my projects to be better; Drew Galaska, Steve Rybinski, Erin Rybinski, and P.J. Starks for their candid advice; Nathan Carroll, who helped connect me with Simon Barrett; Matt Rassmussen, whose unyielding passion for all things horror is an inspiration; Marin Christensen, Chris "Brownie" Brown, Lance Karasti, Emily McNeil, Randall Oelerich, Samuel T. Weston and Brandon Cole, whose experience in film helped dictate the book's direction; Dillion Timm, for his inspirational art; JoAnn Baker, who showed me that writing a book is a thing that can be done.

INDEX

Made in the USA
Middletown, DE
16 May 2021